How to Make Your First $1000 with AI in 30 Days

By

Harry Madu

Table of Contents

About the Author

Harry Madu is a writer, entrepreneur, and practical educator focused on helping everyday people use technology to create real income and real freedom. Through clear, encouraging guidance, he has helped beginners cut through confusion, build confidence, and take their first steps toward earning online with simple, useful AI-powered skills.

With a talent for turning complicated ideas into plain, actionable advice, Harry writes for people who are motivated but overwhelmed, curious but cautious, and ready to improve their lives without needing a perfect background, big budget, or technical experience.

How to Make Your First $1,000 with AI in 30 Days (No Experience, No Money Needed) was written to prove that the opportunity is real, but only for those willing to approach it with honesty, effort, and a willingness to start small. The author believes that AI is not a shortcut to success, but a tool that can help ordinary people move faster, serve better, and open doors that once felt out of reach.

When not writing, Harry Madu is usually exploring new digital business ideas, studying human behaviour, and finding better ways to help people turn uncertainty into momentum.

Dedication

This book is dedicated to beginners.

To the person who feels behind.

To the one who has doubted themselves more times than they can count.
To the one who is tired of watching opportunity pass by and wondering whether it is meant for other people.

It is.

This book is for anyone who has ever needed a second chance, a first win, or a reason to believe that change is still possible.

May these pages help you start.

Acknowledgement

This book was written for ordinary people trying to do something brave: improve their lives in a world that changes faster every year.

Thank you to the learners, beginners, freelancers, creators, and quiet strivers who keep showing up even when they are uncertain, discouraged, or starting with very little. Your persistence is more powerful than you realise. The questions you ask, the fears you carry, and the hopes you hold are what shaped this book.

Thank you as well to the thinkers, builders, teachers, and innovators whose work has made AI more accessible to everyday people. New tools matter, but what matters even more is helping people use them wisely, ethically, and with purpose.

To friends, supporters, and everyone who believes that practical knowledge can change a life: thank you. Encouragement matters. A timely word can keep someone going long enough to change their future.

And finally, thank you to the reader for picking up this book. Your willingness to learn, act, and begin before you feel fully ready is what this book is all about.

I   hope   it   helps   you   earn   more   than   money. I hope it helps you earn momentum, self-trust, and a new sense of possibility.

If you want, I can also turn these into a more personal, warm, and named version if you share the author's name and the tone you want.

Introduction

You Are Not Lazy, Broken, or "Bad at Business"

What does this book understand about the reader?

- Feeling financially stressed and mentally exhausted
- Wanting extra income but not knowing where to begin
- Being sceptical because so many online promises feel fake
- Feeling embarrassed about having "no skills" or "no experience"
- Fearing technology, sales, rejection, and wasting time

What makes this book different?

- No hype, no overnight-rich promises
- No need to code, build an audience, or spend money
- Focus on simple services and small wins first
- Built for action, not information overload
- A 30-day path designed for momentum, not perfection

What can the reader expect?

- A realistic 30-day roadmap
- Beginner-friendly tools and workflows
- Simple income methods that can work fast
- Scripts, examples, and decision-making help
- A path they can repeat long after the first $1,000

The truth about making money with AI:

- AI is not magic; it is a speed and leverage tool

- People do not pay for AI itself—they pay for outcomes
- Beginners can earn by solving small, clear problems
- The first $1,000 usually comes from service, not scale
- Confidence comes after action, not before it

Chapter 1: Why Most Beginners Stay Stuck, and How to Escape Fast

Let me guess.

You've spent hours watching videos about making money online. Maybe even days. You've seen people talk about AI like it's some magic machine that prints cash while you sleep. You've heard about freelancing, content creation, prompt selling, digital products, automation, faceless channels, and side hustles with names you barely understand.

And yet, here you are.

Still stuck.

Still unsure where to begin.
Still wondering whether this works for others, but somehow won't work for you.
Still feeling that quiet frustration of wanting your life to change… but not knowing where to start.

That feeling can weigh heavily on you.

It's not just confusion. It's heavier than that. It's the pressure of needing money, mixed with the fear of wasting your time. It's opening your phone to "figure things out" and closing it an hour later, feeling even worse than before. It's wanting a way forward so badly, but feeling frozen every time you try to choose one.

If that's where you are, I want you to hear this clearly:

You are not lazy.
You are not too late.
You are not too inexperienced.
And you are definitely not the only one who feels this way.

Most beginners don't stay stuck because they aren't capable. They stay stuck because they are trying to move through noise, fear, and bad advice all at once.

This chapter is about changing that.

Not with hype. Not with fake motivation. Not with empty "believe in yourself" quotes.

We're going to strip this down to something simple, honest, and workable, so you can stop circling the idea of making money with AI and start taking your first real steps toward it.

Reality Check

Before you earn anything, you need to understand what's actually keeping you stuck.

Because it usually isn't a lack of opportunity.

It's a set of beliefs that sound reasonable on the surface, but quietly keep people in research mode, fear mode, and waiting mode for months.

Sometimes years.

Let's deal with the three biggest lies first.

The First Lie: "I Need a Big Audience"

This one stops a lot of potential talent before it ever begins.

They think, "Who would buy from me? I don't have followers. I'm not famous. I don't have a personal brand."

So instead of offering a service, they spend weeks trying to look established. They tweak their bio. They think about logos. They wonder if they need a website. They tell themselves they'll start once they look more professional.

But your first income probably won't come from being popular.

It will come from being useful.

That's an important difference.

A local business owner who is too busy to write captions for social media does not care whether you have ten followers or ten thousand. A job seeker who is embarrassed by their résumé does not need you to be famous. They need help. A self-employed person drowning in unfinished tasks does not need a polished brand. They need someone who can take the problem off their plate.

People pay for outcomes.

They pay for relief.
They pay for saved time.

They pay for clearer words, better presentation, less stress, and faster progress.

Your first client is not looking for a celebrity. They are looking for someone who can help.

The Second Lie: "I Need Special Skills First"

This one sounds responsible, which is why it's so dangerous.

It tells you to wait until you're more prepared. Learn more. Watch more. Practice more. Build your confidence first.

Now, to be fair, yes, you do need skills. But not the enormous array of skills the internet suggests you require.

You do not need to master copywriting, design, sales psychology, automation, coding, marketing strategy, content systems, branding, and advanced AI workflows before you can make your first dollar.

That is not preparation. That is avoidance in a nicer outfit.

What you need is one usable skill.

Just one.

Can you use AI to help draft social captions for a small business? Can you use it to rewrite a résumé so it sounds stronger and clearer? Can you turn messy notes into a clean email, blog outline, or basic content draft?

Can you help someone go from disorganised to finished?

That's enough to start.

Not enough to build a giant company overnight. Enough to begin. And beginning matters more than people realise.

Because real skill grows faster in action than it does in theory.

You learn more from doing three small jobs than from watching thirty more tutorials.

The Third Lie: "I Need Money to Make Money"

There was a time when this felt truer.

If you wanted to start something online, you often needed software, ad spend, paid tools, hosting, and a bunch of subscriptions before you could even test an idea. That made the whole thing feel closed off to ordinary people.

But AI has changed the entry point.

Today, a beginner can start with free or low-cost tools and offer simple services without building a giant setup at first. You can draft, research, rewrite, brainstorm, organise, and create much faster than people could even a few years ago.

That doesn't mean success is automatic. It isn't.

But it does mean the gate is no longer locked the way it used to be.

For most people, the real problem is not the lack of money.

It's the lack of focus.

It's second-guessing every move.

It's getting excited, then overwhelmed.

It's trying five ideas halfway instead of one idea properly.

The good news is that focus costs nothing.

And if you can build that, you can get further than people with better tools but weaker discipline.

Why AI Creates a Real Opportunity for Ordinary Beginners

Let's be honest about what AI is and what it isn't.

AI is not a shortcut around effort.
It is not a guarantee of income.
And it is definitely not a replacement for common sense, judgment, or human care.

What it is, though, is leverage.

It helps you work faster. It helps you start from something instead of starting from nothing. It helps beginners produce rough drafts, ideas, structures, and first versions in minutes instead of hours.

That matters more than you think.

Because when you are new, one of the hardest parts is momentum. Everything feels slow. Every task feels bigger than it is. You spend more energy figuring out how to begin than actually doing the work.

AI lowers that friction.

Instead of staring at a blank page, you have a draft to improve. Instead of struggling to find words, you have material to shape. Instead of feeling lost, you finally have a starting point.

That gives ordinary people a shot they didn't have before.

Not because the work disappears—but because the path into the work becomes less intimidating.

And when the path feels less intimidating, more people actually take the first step.

The Beginner Advantage Nobody Talks About

You may feel behind right now, but beginners have strengths too.

You probably don't see them because all you can feel is what you lack. But that's not the whole picture.

You also have speed.

You don't have a complicated system to maintain. You don't have a team to manage. You don't have old habits slowing you down. You can choose an offer today, test it tomorrow, and improve it next week.

You have flexibility.

You are not locked into one business model. You can try simple services, listen to feedback, and shift quickly without tearing down a giant machine.

And you have low overhead.

That part matters a lot.

If you're not carrying huge costs, you don't need a giant breakthrough. You don't need a single viral moment or a massive client. You just need enough momentum to start stacking small wins.

Think about that.

A $50 service sold 20 times is $1,000.
A $100 service sold 10 times is $1,000.
A $250 service sold 4 times is $1,000.

That first $1,000 becomes much less mysterious when you stop imagining some dramatic online success story and start thinking in terms of repeatable, useful work.

That is how this gets real.

Why Trying to Learn Everything Is the Fastest Way to Fail

This is the trap smart people fall into.

Because smart people know there's a lot they don't know. So they keep learning.

And learning feels productive. It feels safe. It feels responsible.

But there comes a point where learning becomes a hiding place.

You watch another video because you still don't feel ready.

You save another thread in case you need it later.

You open five tabs, compare ten ideas, and call it research.

Meanwhile, nothing changes.

No offer.

No outreach.

No first client.

No proof.

Just more information and more mental clutter.

The internet makes money from keeping you invested. It does not get paid when you become focused.

That's why there is endless content teaching you what is possible, but far less content that forces you to choose one path and stick to it.

But income comes from repetition, not fascination.

You do not need ten business models.

You need one simple offer which you can explain in one sentence.

That sentence might be:

"I create ready-to-post social captions for local businesses."

Or:

"I help job seekers rewrite their résumés and cover letters."

Or:

"I turn rough notes into clean content drafts for occupied business owners."

That kind of clarity is powerful because people understand it immediately.

And when people understand what you do, they are far more likely to buy it from you.

The Simple Formula That Actually Works

Here is the formula I want burned into your mind:

Solve a problem, offer a result, repeat.

That's it.

Simple enough to sound obvious. Strong enough to build income.

You do not need to impress people with jargon.
You do not need to create a complicated business.
You do not need to become "an expert in AI."

You need to help someone get from a frustrating before-state to a better after-state.

A business owner is tired of never knowing what to post. You help by creating captions.
A job seeker feels embarrassed by their résumé. You help by rewriting it.
A freelancer has ideas but no time to turn them into content. You help by organising and drafting it.

That is real value.

And after the first time, you do it again. Then again. Then better.

This is where confidence actually comes from—not from motivation, but from evidence.

How to Stop Consuming and Start Earning

At some point, you have to stop asking, "What else should I learn?" and start asking, "What can I help someone with, this week?"

That question changes your whole posture.

It pulls you out of passive mode and into practical mode.

Instead of collecting more information, you begin looking for problems to offer solutions.
Instead of admiring other people's success, you start building your own proof.
Instead of trying to understand everything, you focus on one result you can deliver.

This is where many people hesitate, because action feels riskier than learning.

Learning protects your ego.

Action exposes you.

Once you send an offer, you can be ignored.
Once you make a sample, it can feel imperfect.

Once you put yourself out there, you lose the comfort of "I'm still getting ready."

But that discomfort is where the progress begins.

The sooner you can make peace with that, the faster you move.

The 30-Day Survival Mindset: Progress Over Perfection

For the next 30 days, I want you to think differently.

You are not trying to build a perfect business.
You are trying to create momentum.

That means your standard is not perfection. Your standard is movement.

You do not need the perfect offer.
You do not need the perfect profile.
You do not need the perfect niche, the perfect plan, or the perfect confidence.

You need a direction.
You need a small offer.
You need a reason to act today.

This is what I call the survival mindset.

No panic. No desperation. Just a refusal to waste another month standing still.

In this mindset, messy action beats clean hesitation.

A basic offer sent out is more valuable than a perfect idea that remains only in your head.

An imperfect sample is better than endless planning.

A beginner's first client is better than an expert's unfinished dream.

If you remember nothing else from this chapter, remember this:

Progress creates proof. Proof creates belief.

Not the other way around.

You do not believe first and then act boldly. Most of the time, you act nervously, get a small result, and then begin to believe.

That is how it works in real life.

What This Looks Like in the Real World

Let's bring this down in simple terms.

Example 1: Simple Social Captions for a Local Business

Imagine a woman named Sarah.

She's not a marketing expert. She doesn't have fancy credentials. She's just under pressure financially and tired of feeling like everyone else knows how to make money online except her.

One day, she notices something obvious: lots of local businesses have decent products but weak social media presence. Their pages are inactive, inconsistent, or full of rushed posts that clearly weren't planned.

So she chooses a simple service.

She uses AI to help brainstorm caption ideas, create post themes, and draft content for a local café. Then she edits it so it sounds human, relevant, and usable.

Her offer is basic:

"I create ready-to-post social captions for local businesses."

That's it.

She's not promising to triple revenue. She's not pretending to be a full agency. She's only solving one small but annoying problem.

A few people ignore her. One says no. Another says, "What do you charge?"

That question changes something in her.

Because now it's no longer a fantasy in her head. It's real.

Example 2: AI-Assisted Résumé Rewrites for Job Seekers

Now picture Daniel.

He's not a career coach. He's not some polished LinkedIn expert. But he knows how many people struggle to talk about themselves clearly, especially when they're applying for jobs and already feeling insecure.

So he chooses another simple offer.

He uses AI to improve résumé summaries, strengthen bullet points, and help draft cover letters. But he doesn't blindly trust the output.

He checks it, cleans it up, and makes sure it sounds natural and truthful.

His offer is:

"I help job seekers improve their résumés and cover letters so they sound clearer and more confident."

Simple. Useful. Easy to understand.

And that's the pattern you need to see.

Neither Sarah nor Daniel needed a big audience. Neither needed to master everything. Neither needed a huge investment.

They just needed one useful offer and the willingness to test it.

Step-by-Step Action Plan

Now let's make this practical.

Not "someday." Today.

Here's how to break out of stuck mode.

Step 1: Write Down the Beliefs You're Done Carrying

Take a piece of paper or open the notes app and write these three lines:

- I do not need a big audience to earn my first money.
- I do not need to know everything before I begin.
- I do not need a lot of money to start.

This may sound too simple to matter. Do it anyway.

What stays vague tends to control you. What gets named loses some of its power.

Step 2: Choose One Small Problem You Can Help Solve

Pick one.

Not three. Not six. Just One.

Choose a problem that feels simple and useful, not glamorous.

Here are some strong beginner-friendly options:

- writing social media captions for local businesses
- rewriting résumés for job seekers
- drafting product descriptions for small sellers
- creating simple email sequences
- turning messy notes into clean summaries or content drafts
- brainstorming blog or content ideas for busy business owners

Do not overthink this choice. You are not choosing your life's work. You are choosing your first test.

That is a much lighter decision.

Step 3: Turn It Into a Clear One-Sentence Offer

Use this formula:

I help [specific person] get [specific result] without [specific frustration].

Examples:

I help local businesses get ready-to-post captions without spending hours writing them.

I help job seekers improve their résumés without struggling over what to say.

I help busy creators turn rough ideas into polished drafts without having to start from scratch.

Notice what these offers do well: they are clear, narrow, and easy to understand.

Confused people do not buy. Clear people do.

Step 4: Make One Sample Today

Before you try to get a client, prove to yourself that you can create something useful.

If your offer is social captions, create 10 sample captions for a café, gym, or barbershop.

If your offer is résumé rewriting, take a sample résumé and improve the summary and bullet points.

If your offer is email writing, draft a welcome email and one follow-up message for a pretend business.

Use AI to help you move faster, but do not stop there. Edit what it gives you. Make it sound real. Tighten weak lines. Remove generic fluff.

Your value is not in pressing a button.

Your value is in turning a rough AI output into something a real person can actually use.

Step 5: Make a List of Five People or Businesses Who Could Need This

This part matters because it pulls you out of theory.

Look around you.

Find five real people or businesses who genuinely might benefit from your offer.

That could include:

- local businesses with weak or inconsistent social media
- friends or relatives who are job hunting
- online sellers with poor product descriptions
- freelancers or coaches who always seem too busy to post content
- small service businesses that clearly need help communicating better

Do not worry about whether they will say yes. That is not the point yet.

The point is to connect your offer to real people, not imaginary future customers.

Step 6: Send One Honest Message

Not a perfect message. An honest one.

Here's an example for social captions:

"Hi, I noticed your business has great reviews and a strong local presence, but your social media seems a bit inconsistent. I'm helping small businesses create ready-to-post captions using AI plus human editing, and I've put together a few ideas tailored to your business. Would you like me to send them?"

And for résumé help:

"Hi, I'm helping job seekers improve their résumés and cover letters so they sound clearer and more professional. I know applying for jobs can be frustrating, so I thought I'd reach out. If you want, I can show you an example of how I'd improve it."

That's enough.

No hard sell. No fake confidence. No pretending to be bigger than you are.

Just clear, respectful outreach.

Step 7: Aim for a Reply, Not a Miracle

Your first goal is not to "close" someone.

It is to start conversations.

A reply is progress.
A question is progress.
A maybe is progress.

Because every real interaction teaches you something useful:

- what people understand immediately
- what confuses them

- what they care about most
- what words make your offer stronger

Beginners often expect instant results and feel defeated immediately. Don't do that.

Treat your first outreach like market research with potential upside.

Step 8: Start Small When Someone Says Yes

When interest comes, keep it simple.

Do not overwhelm people with giant packages.

Offer a starter version.

Maybe that means:

- 10 captions instead of 30
- one résumé rewrite instead of a full "career package"
- three product descriptions instead of twenty
- one week of content instead of a monthly retainer

Small first jobs are good for both of you.

They lower the risk for the client and lower the pressure on you. They help you get proof, testimonials, and experience without needing to be perfect.

Step 9: Repeat Before You Reinvent

This is where momentum is built.

Once you find an offer people respond to, even a little, stay with it long enough to learn from it.

Don't quit after three days because another opportunity looks more exciting.

New ideas are seductive because they let you start over without facing the discomfort of repetition.

But repetition is where money lives.

The more times you solve the same kind of problem, the faster and better you get. The faster and better you get, the easier it becomes to earn.

That is how small services turn into real income.

Common Mistakes to Avoid

Watching Endless Tutorials

There is a point where "learning" becomes procrastination with better branding.

Be careful.

You can watch helpful content, yes. But the moment it starts replacing action, it becomes part of the problem.

A good rule is this: for every 30 minutes you spend learning, spend at least 30 minutes doing.

Jumping Between Ideas Every Day

This kills momentum faster than almost anything else.

One day, it's freelancing.

The next day, it's digital products.

Then it's affiliate marketing.

Then faceless videos.

Then prompt packs.

Then automation.

By the end of the week, you have a crowded brain and nothing to show for it.

Stick with one simple path long enough to get honest feedback from the real world.

Waiting to Feel Ready

You may never feel ready in the clean, confident way you imagine.

Most people start shaky.

They send the message with doubt.
They make the sample while second-guessing themselves.
They price the offer nervously.
They improve as they go.

That's normal.

Readiness is often the result of action, not the requirement for it.

Making Your Offer Too Vague

"AI help for businesses" is not an offer. It is a blurry category.

People respond better when they can picture the result.

Say what you do in plain language:

- Instagram captions
- résumé rewrites
- product descriptions
- blog outlines
- follow-up emails

Specific offers feel safer to buy because the buyer understands what they're getting.

Letting AI Do All the Thinking

This is a mistake a lot of beginners make.

They paste in a prompt, get an output, and assume the job is done.

It isn't.

AI can give you speed. It can give you a starting point. It can help you break through blank-page anxiety. But it still needs your judgment.

You need to notice weak phrases.
You need to cut fluff.
You need to personalise the work.
You need to make sure it actually fits the person or business you're helping.

That final layer is what makes the output worth paying for.

Quick Win Task

Before this day ends, do this:

Choose one offer.
Write it in one sentence.
Create one sample.
Send one message.

That's your assignment.

Not to "build a brand."
Not to spend three hours researching tools.
Not to redesign your profile picture.

Just this:

One offer.
One sample.
One real message.

That may not sound like much, but it is more powerful than another week of overthinking.

Because action breaks the spell of being trapped/stuck.

The moment you do something real, the fog starts to lift.

You do not need a new personality to succeed at this.

You do not need to become flashy, loud, ultra-confident, or hyper-technical. You do not need to act like the people online who make everything sound easy.

You just need to become someone who acts before they feel fully ready.

That is the shift.

The people who make progress are not always smarter. Often, they are just more willing to be beginners in public. More willing to send the imperfect message. More willing to test a simple offer. More willing to learn by doing instead of hiding in preparation.

That can be you.

And no, it may not happen instantly. You may get ignored. You may send messages that go nowhere. You may feel awkward at first.

Welcome to real life.

That does not mean it isn't working. It means you have finally left the sidelines.

Your first $1,000 will not come from having all the answers.

It will come from solving simple problems for real people, one step at a time.

So don't leave this chapter inspired but unchanged.

Do the uncomfortable thing.

Pick one problem.
Offer one result.
Send one message.

That is how people escape stuck mode.

That is how momentum begins.

And that is how this book stops being something you read, and starts becoming something you live.

Chapter 2: The Truth About AI Income: What Works, What Doesn't, and What to Avoid

Let's tell the truth right away.

Most people who are curious about making money through AI are not lazy. They are not stupid. They are not "behind."

They are tired.

Tired of being stretched.
Tired of needing extra income.
Tired of hearing the same recycled promises from people who seem to make more money selling the dream than doing the work.

Maybe that is where you are right now.

You want to believe there is a real opportunity here. You also do not want to get played.

You have probably seen the videos:
"Make passive income with one AI prompt."
"Earn $10,000 this month with no skills."
"Start an AI business in one afternoon."

And part of you wants it to be true, because life would feel a lot lighter if it were.

But another part of you knows better.

You know that when something sounds too easy, there is usually a catch. You know that the internet is full of people who talk fast, show screenshots, and leave out the messy middle where actual work happens.

So this chapter is here to do something simple and important:

Cut through the noise.

Not to kill your hope. To protect it.

Because AI can help you make money. It really can. But not in the fantasy way people sell online. The real opportunity is quieter than that. Less flashy. Less glamorous. And much more useful.

It does not start with chasing "passive income."
It starts with learning how to become helpful.

That is the part people skip.
That is also the part that gets paid.

If you understand that now, you will save yourself weeks of distraction, false starts, and discouragement. You will stop looking for magic and start building something that actually has a chance of working.

And when money is tight, that matters.

You do not need more hype.
You need a clear path you can trust.

Reality Check

AI is not your business.

AI is your tool.

That one shift in thinking will save you a lot of confusion.

A tool has no value on its own. It becomes valuable when you use it to solve a real problem for a real person. A hammer matters because it helps build something. A calculator matters because it helps solve something faster. AI is no different.

So when people say, "Make money with AI," what they usually mean is one of two things:

Either they are talking about using AI to help someone get a result faster, or they are talking nonsense.

That may sound blunt, but it is important.

Because beginners waste a huge amount of time asking the wrong question:

"How do I make money with AI?"

A better question is:

"What can I help people do better, faster, or more easily with AI?"

That question leads to real opportunities.

What AI can realistically help beginners do

If you are starting with no audience, no business experience, and no technical background, AI can still be incredibly useful.

It can help you:

- turn a blank page into a first draft
- rewrite awkward wording into cleaner language
- organise ideas that feel messy in your head
- summarise information quickly
- turn long content into short content
- generate options when you are stuck
- speed up repetitive writing tasks
- help you create templates, checklists, captions, summaries, and basic drafts faster

That is not small. That is a real advantage.

Imagine a woman who runs a tiny candle business from home. She is good at making products. She is not good at writing product descriptions or social captions. Every time she tries, she gets frustrated and puts it off.

Now imagine you help her by using AI to draft descriptions, then rewriting them so they actually sound clear, warm, and specific to her products. She gets better listings. Her shop looks more polished. She feels relieved.

That is value.

Or picture a man applying for jobs after being laid off. He has real experience, but his résumé is weak. It sounds flat. His cover letters feel stiff. He is already discouraged, and every application feels heavier than it should.

You use AI to help reshape his résumé bullets, tighten his wording, and draft a cover letter he can actually use as a base. Suddenly, he sounds more confident on paper. He feels less embarrassed about hitting "apply."

That is valuable too.

This is where beginners can win: not by building some complicated AI empire, but by helping ordinary people with ordinary problems they already have.

What AI cannot do for you?

Now let's be equally honest about the other side.

AI cannot replace judgment.
It cannot build trust for you.
It cannot promise results.
It cannot understand nuance the way a real person can.
And it absolutely cannot do all the work while you sit back and collect money.

This is where a lot of people get disappointed.

They assume the tool is smart enough to do the thinking for them.
So, they copy the first answer it gives, paste it into a document, and think they have created something valuable.

Usually, they have not.

AI often gives you something that looks polished at first glance but falls apart on closer inspection. It can sound smooth while saying nothing. It can be vague, repetitive, and weirdly hollow. It can miss context. It can make things up. It can give the same generic answer to ten different people and pretend it is personalised.

That is why you cannot use AI mindlessly.

You have to guide it.
Shape it.
Check it.
Fix what is weak.
Throw out what sounds fake.
Add the human judgment that makes the final result useful.

The simplest way to think about it is this:

AI is a fast assistant.
Not a miracle worker.

Helpful? Absolutely.
Perfect? Not even close.

Why "passive income on day one" is the wrong goal

This part matters because it is where many beginners lose months.

When people are stressed about money, "passive income" sounds like the dream. Of course, it does. The idea of making money without constantly trading time for it feels like freedom. It feels like an escape.

But for most beginners, chasing passive income first is a mistake.

Not because passive income is fake.

Because it usually comes later.

A digital product that sells while you sleep still has to be created well. It has to solve a specific problem. It has to be positioned properly. It has to reach the right people. A content business that eventually earns through ads, affiliates, or offers still needs time, trust, consistency, and attention.

None of that is impossible.

It is just slower than people admit.

When you need your first few hundred dollars—or your first thousand—the faster path is usually direct service.

Why?

Because you do not need a crowd.

You need one person.

One person with a problem.

One offer that helps.

One conversation.

One payment.

That is a much shorter road than trying to build an audience big enough to support "passive" income before you have even made your first sale.

Passive income is not the starting line.

It is often the result of skills, proof, and repetition built over time.

The fastest path to first income: AI-assisted services

If your main goal is to make your first money, not impress strangers online, start here.

AI-assisted services are usually the fastest path because they are simple to understand and easy to sell. You are not asking someone to believe in a vague future outcome. You are helping them with a clear task that they already need done.

You are not selling "AI."
You are selling relief.

For example:

- a month of social media captions for a small business owner
- a résumé and cover letter refresh for a job seeker
- product description rewrites for an Etsy seller
- repurposed posts from a podcast episode or video
- a drafted email newsletter for a busy coach or freelancer
- a clean lead list for someone doing outreach
- a printable or template bundle for a specific audience
- a short research summary for a busy professional

Notice how grounded these are.

No buzzwords.
No futuristic nonsense.
Just useful work.

A local fitness coach may not care about AI at all. What she cares about is this: she has clients, classes, messages, and a hundred other things to do. She does not want to spend Saturday afternoon writing captions for next week's posts.

If you can make her life easier, you are valuable.

That is how you need to think.

The second path: simple digital products with clear demand

Digital products can work well too, especially once you understand real problems people will pay to solve.

But there is a big catch.

Most beginners create digital products that are easy to make, not products people actually need.

That is why the internet is full of beautiful, useless downloads.

Generic planners.
Generic prompt packs.
Generic journals.
Generic templates for problems nobody urgently wants fixed.

AI makes it even easier to create these quickly, which is exactly why you need to be careful. Faster creation does not automatically mean better business.

A weak idea produced faster is still a weak idea.

A simple digital product works when it is specific and practical.

For example:

- a customer response template pack for Etsy sellers
- a first-job résumé worksheet for college students
- a weekly meal planner for busy parents on a budget
- a follow-up email swipe file for service providers
- a content planning template for real estate agents
- an interview prep checklist for remote job seekers

These are not exciting in a flashy way. They are exciting in the only way that matters:

They are useful.

The slower path: content-based income and why it should not be Plan A

Now, let's talk about the path that gets romanticised the most.

Content-based income.

YouTube channels.
TikTok pages.
Blogs.
Newsletters.
Affiliate content.
Personal brands.

Yes, this can absolutely turn into real income.
But for most beginners, it should not be your first plan.

Because content usually pays late.

You can post for weeks and earn nothing.

You can be consistent and still feel invisible.

You can work hard and get little traction while you are still learning what people care about.

That does not mean content is bad. It means content is slower than direct service. It is better used as support, not as your main strategy when you need income now.

A lot of people hide inside content because it feels safer.

Posting tips feels easier than making an offer.
Designing brand graphics feels easier than reaching out to someone.
Talking about business feels easier than doing business.

But safe does not always mean effective.

If you need momentum, let content support your work. Share examples. Show helpful tips. Build trust. But do not rely on content alone to rescue you financially in the beginning.

What ethical AI income looks like?

This chapter would not be complete without talking about ethics, because this is one reason many people feel uneasy around AI income in the first place.

They do not want to be scammy.
They do not want to fake expertise.
They do not want to mislead people.

Good. Hold onto that.

Ethical AI income is not complicated.

It means you use AI to help you deliver useful work—not to trick people, copy people, or pretend you did something you did not do.

It means:

- you review what you deliver
- you do not promise things you cannot control
- you do not fake qualifications
- you do not pass off lazy, generic output as premium work
- you do not use AI to spam people or manipulate them
- you do not take money for tasks you cannot responsibly complete

Using AI is not unethical.
Using it carelessly can be.

The standard is simple:
Is the final result honest, helpful, and worth paying for?

If the answer is yes, you are on solid ground.

How to avoid shady shortcuts and empty promises

Here is a rule that will protect you:

If the business model depends more on hype than usefulness, stay away from it.

That includes:

- selling impossible income dreams to desperate people

- pretending one prompt equals a business
- mass-producing generic junk and calling it premium
- spamming strangers with copy-paste outreach
- copying someone else's offer and changing two words
- buying overpriced "secret system" courses that never show real execution
- obsessing over looking successful instead of becoming useful

A real opportunity often looks less exciting than a fake one.

That is one of the reasons people miss it.

The truth is usually plain.

People pay when you help them save time, reduce stress, communicate better, organise faster, or make something clearer.

That is the foundation.
Not hype.
Not tricks.
Not screenshots.

Usefulness.

Solution Breakdown

Now let's make this practical.

Here are beginner-friendly ways to make money with AI that are grounded, understandable, and realistic.

1. AI-assisted social media caption packs

This is one of the easiest entry points because the pain is obvious. Many small business owners know they should post regularly. They just do not want to write the captions.

You can help by creating a batch of captions for them using AI as a drafting tool, then editing the content so it sounds natural, relevant, and specific to their business.

What you are really selling is not "content."
You are selling consistency and saved time.

A hairdresser does not wake up wanting "AI-powered social strategy."
She wants next week's posts done so she can focus on her clients.

That difference matters.

2. Résumé and cover letter upgrades

This is a strong beginner offer because the result is easy for people to understand.

You are helping someone present themselves better on paper.

AI can help you rewrite weak bullet points, improve phrasing, tailor a cover letter, and make the overall document feel stronger and more professional. Your job is to make sure it stays truthful, specific, and aligned with the person's actual experience.

You are not inventing achievements.
You are helping real strengths come through more clearly.

For someone who already feels rejected and discouraged, that can mean a lot.

3. Product description writing for small sellers

Many small sellers are excellent at what they make and terrible at describing it.

That is not an insult. It is just reality.

They know their product so well that they often write from inside their own head instead of from the customer's point of view. Or they rush through the description because they are juggling everything else, too.

You can use AI to help draft product descriptions, benefit-focused bullet points, and clearer wording. Then you refine it so it sounds believable, specific, and appealing.

You are helping a product look worth buying.

4. Short-form content repurposing

This is one of the best beginner services because so much valuable content already exists in long form.

A business owner records a podcast.

A coach does a live video.

A consultant writes a long post.

A creator uploads a YouTube video.

Most of them never squeeze all the value out of that content.

You can.

You can turn one long piece into several shorter pieces: captions, quote posts, short scripts, bullet summaries, newsletter snippets, or post ideas.

AI helps you move faster. Your value comes from organising the material well and shaping it into assets the client can actually use.

5. Basic email or newsletter drafting

A lot of business owners know they should email their audience, but they freeze when it is time to write.

They do not know what to say.
They overthink it.
They put it off.

That is where you can help.

You can draft welcome emails, weekly newsletters, product announcements, follow-up emails, or simple promotional messages. AI can help structure the first version. You step in to make it clearer, warmer, and more human.

You are not just writing emails.
You are helping someone stay in touch with the people who may buy from them.

6. Lead list building and outreach support

This is less glamorous, but extremely practical.

Many freelancers, service providers, and small businesses need help finding potential leads and organising outreach. They need names, websites, emails, notes, and perhaps a first message draft.

If you are detail-oriented, this can be a strong beginner offer.

AI can help you draft outreach messages and speed up some research tasks. But this only works if you do it ethically. No spam blasts. No fake personalisation. No shady data scraping. Keep it clean, targeted, and useful.

7. Printable or template creation with AI help

Templates and printables work best when they solve a clear, narrow problem.

Think less "life planner for everyone" and more "new client onboarding checklist for freelance designers" or "weekly meal planner for busy moms trying to cut grocery costs."

AI can help you brainstorm sections, draft content, and organise ideas. You turn that into something easy to use, visually clean, and actually worth downloading.

8. Simple research summaries for busy professionals

This is another underrated opportunity.

A lot of people do not need more information. They need less chaos.

Busy professionals often want a topic explained clearly without having to dig through ten tabs, long reports, or scattered articles. You can help by creating short summaries, briefing notes, overviews, or easy-to-read snapshots.

AI can help you process information faster, but you still need to verify, simplify, and structure it properly.

That human step is what makes it valuable.

Step-by-Step Action Plan

Let's turn all of this into something you can actually do.

Not next month.
Today.

Step 1: Stop chasing "AI opportunities" and start looking for problems

Write down three types of people you could realistically help.

For example:

- small business owners
- job seekers
- Etsy sellers
- freelancers
- coaches
- busy professionals

Now write one annoying problem each group already has.

Examples:

- "I never know what to post."

- "My résumé sounds weak."
- "I hate writing product descriptions."
- "I have content, but no time to repurpose it."
- "I should send emails, but I keep avoiding it."

This exercise matters because it forces you to stop thinking like a spectator and start thinking like a problem-solver.

Step 2: Choose one path only

You do not need three business models right now.
You need one.

Choose one of these:

- AI-assisted service
- simple digital product
- content-based income

If you want the fastest chance of earning, choose an AI-assisted service.

That is the path with the shortest distance between effort and money.

Step 3: Pick one offer you can explain in one sentence

Do not overcomplicate this.

Here are examples:

- "I help small businesses get social media captions drafted for the month."
- "I help job seekers improve their résumés and cover letters."

- "I help online sellers rewrite product descriptions so their listings sound clearer."
- "I turn one long video into multiple short social posts."
- "I draft simple newsletters for busy business owners."

If your offer sounds vague, simplify it until a tired person could understand it in five seconds.

Step 4: Create one sample

Do not build a whole website.
Do not design a logo.
Do not spend hours choosing fonts.

Make one proof-of-work sample.

If you picked social media captions, create ten sample captions for a local business.
If you picked résumé help, rewrite one sample résumé section.
If you picked product descriptions, redo three listings.
If you picked research summaries, make a one-page summary on a useful topic.

One sample is enough to start.

Step 5: Use AI like an assistant, not a substitute

Here is a better workflow:

1. Give AI context about the person, business, or task.
2. Ask for a rough draft or ideas.
3. Pull out the strongest parts.

4. Rewrite what sounds generic.

5. Remove fluff.

6. Add specifics.

7. Fact-check anything important.

8. Read it out loud and make it sound like a real person wrote it.

That last step matters more than most people realise.

If it sounds robotic to you, it will sound robotic to the client as well.

Step 6: Reach out to one real person

Not fifty.
One.

Send a simple, low-pressure message.

For example:

"Hi, I've been practising helping small businesses create social media captions faster. I put together a sample so you can see the style. Thought I'd share it in case this would save you some time."

Or:

"Hi, I'm helping job seekers improve their résumés and cover letters so they sound clearer and stronger. If that would be useful to you, I'd be happy to help."

You are not trying to sound like a giant company.
You are trying to be helpful and clear.

Step 7: Price for momentum

At the beginning, your goal is not to maximise every dollar.

Your goal is to get a yes.
To do the work.
To get proof.
To build confidence.

That might mean starting with a smaller project or a beginner-friendly price point while you learn. There is nothing wrong with that as long as you do not stay stuck there forever.

What matters now is movement.

Step 8: Pay attention to what people respond to

Listen carefully when someone reacts positively.

They may not say, "Your writing is excellent."
They may say, "This saves me so much time."
Or, "This makes the whole thing feel less overwhelming."

That is gold.

Those words tell you what people actually value. Use that language when describing your offer in the future.

Step 9: Ignore everything that does not help you get your first sale

For now, you do not need:

- a personal brand strategy

- a complex funnel

- premium software

- a website

- a perfect portfolio

- ten offers

- a content calendar

- a complicated automation setup

You need one useful offer, one decent sample, and one honest conversation.

That is enough.

Common Mistakes to Avoid

Selling "AI" instead of selling the result

Most people do not care which tool you used.
They care what problem gets solved.

Do not say:
"I use AI to generate optimised digital assets."

Say:
"I help you get your product descriptions written faster."

Clear beats clever every time.

Picking a method because it sounds exciting

A method being trendy does not make it good for you.

You are not trying to win a popularity contest.

You are trying to make money in a way that is realistic, ethical, and manageable.

Choose what fits your current situation, not what gets the most views online.

Copying prompts without understanding the work

A prompt is not a skill.
A prompt is not insight.
A prompt is not a business model.

If you do not understand what makes a good caption, a strong résumé, a useful email, or a solid product description, AI will not save you.

Learn enough to judge quality.
That is where your value comes from.

Overpromising

This can quietly ruin your confidence.

Do not promise guaranteed interviews, guaranteed sales, viral content, or instant growth. Promise the part you can control: clearer writing, faster delivery, stronger positioning, more organised content, and less time wasted.

That is honest.
And honesty compounds.

Hiding inside endless preparation

This is a big one.

You tell yourself you are learning.

You watch another tutorial.

Save another prompt.

Compare another tool.

Outline another plan.

Meanwhile, you still have no offer in front of a real person.

Preparation feels safer than exposure.

But it does not pay.

Action does.

Creating generic products that no one urgently wants

AI makes it easy to create polished-looking junk.

Do not confuse "finished" with "valuable."

Before creating anything, ask:

Who needs this?

What problem does it solve?

Why would someone pay for it?

What makes it genuinely useful?

If you cannot answer those questions clearly, stop and rethink.

Quick Win Task

Set a timer for 30 minutes and do this before the day ends.

Choose one of the beginner-friendly methods from this chapter.

Then write this sentence:

"I help [specific person] get [specific result] without [specific frustration]."

Examples:

"I help small business owners get a month of captions drafted without spending hours trying to think of what to say."

"I help job seekers improve their résumés without struggling to sound professional."

"I help small online sellers rewrite product descriptions without starting from scratch every time."

Next, create one tiny sample based on that offer.

Not a full package.
Not a whole business.
Just one sample.

Then show it to one real person.

That is your assignment.

It may sound small, but this is the kind of step that changes how you feel. You stop being someone who is "thinking about maybe trying AI income someday" and become someone who has actually made something useful.

That shift matters.

You do not need to become a tech genius to make money with AI.

You do not need to know every tool.

You do not need to chase every trend.

You do not need to become an influencer.

And you definitely do not need to fall for the fantasy that money will appear just because a chatbot gave you words.

What you need is simpler than that.

You need to get good at one thing:
using AI to help solve a real problem for a real person.

That is where the money is.
That is where trust is built.
That is where confidence starts to grow.

The internet will keep shouting.
There will always be someone selling shortcuts, screenshots, and easy answers.

Let them.

You are building something sturdier than that.

You are learning how to become useful.
And useful people do not stay stuck forever.

So do not waste your energy trying to find the perfect method.
Pick a real problem.
Choose one simple offer.
Make one small sample.
Help one real person.

That is how this starts.

Not with hype

With honesty.

Not with magic.

With momentum.

And momentum, once it is real, is worth far more than empty
promises.

Chapter 3: Pick Your Path: Choosing the Easiest Route to Your First $1,000

One of the fastest ways to stay broke is to keep "exploring options."

That sounds harsh, but it is true.

When money feels tight, the mind does something strange. It tells you that the safest thing to do is keep looking. Watch one more video. Save one more thread. Compare one more idea. Think a little longer before making a move.

It feels responsible.

It is usually feared to wear smart clothes.

If you have been circling between ideas, starting and stopping, getting excited and then overwhelmed, there is nothing wrong with you. You are not lazy. You are not incapable. You are likely just carrying too much pressure into every decision.

When you need money, choosing one path can feel dangerous. What if this is the wrong one? What if you waste two weeks and get nowhere? What if somebody else picked a better model and you missed your shot?

Those fears make sense. But they also keep people stuck for months.

Here is the truth: for your first $1,000, you do not need the best path in the world.

You need a path you will actually follow.

That is the goal of this chapter. Not to impress you with ten clever income models. Not to throw more options at you. Not to make you feel like you need a personal brand, a huge audience, or some genius business plan.

Just to help you choose one simple, realistic route that fits your life right now.

Because one clear path, followed with focus, beats five exciting ideas that never leave the notes app.

Reality Check

Most beginners do not fail because there are no opportunities.

They fail because they never stay with one long enough to get paid.

They try content writing for three days. Then they see someone selling templates. Then they hear about faceless YouTube channels. Then they wonder if they should start an AI agency. Then they think maybe digital products are more scalable. Then they spend a weekend trying to design a logo for a business they have not even tested.

By the end of the month, they are exhausted, confused, and still at zero.

This is not a strategy problem. It is a focus problem.

The internet rewards novelty. Real income rewards repetition.

The person who picks one useful offer and gets it in front of real people will usually make money faster than the person chasing the "perfect" model.

Especially in the beginning.

Your first $1,000 is not about building your forever business. It is not about maximising leverage or creating seven income streams. It is about proving something important to yourself:

- that you can solve a real problem
- that someone will pay you for it
- that AI can help you work faster and better
- that you are capable of creating momentum

That proof matters more than most people realise.

Once you make your first money, even a small amount, everything changes. You stop guessing. You stop treating this like a theory. You stop asking, "Can this work?" and start asking, "How do I do more of what already works?"

But first, you need to stop scattering your effort.

For the next 30 days, simplicity is your advantage.

Solution Breakdown

Three beginner-friendly paths make sense here. Not thirty. Three.

Each one can work. But they work best for different people and different situations.

1. The Service Model: The Fastest Path

This is the most direct route to your first income.

You use AI to help you deliver a service somebody already needs.

That might mean:

- Rewriting a resume
- drafting a cover letter
- creating social media captions
- turning messy notes into a clean summary
- researching competitors for a small business
- writing email drafts
- repurposing one long video into several short posts
- organising information for someone overwhelmed

The reason this model works so well for beginners is simple: you do not have to build something and hope people buy it later. You find a problem somebody already has, offer to help, and get paid for solving it.

No audience required.
No fancy website required.
No months of setup required.

Just a real problem and a useful offer.

If you need money quickly, this is usually the best place to start.

2. The Product Model: Simple, But Slower to Prove

This model means you create something once and sell it more than once.

That could be:

- a resume template bundle
- interview prep worksheets
- social media caption packs
- a simple Notion planner
- a checklist for job seekers
- a small library of email templates for local businesses

This sounds attractive because it feels more scalable, and it can be. But beginners often fall in love with products for the wrong reason. They want to avoid talking to people.

That is understandable. Products feel safer. You can hide inside the work. Tweak the design. Edit the wording. Keep "improving" it.

But there is a catch: products only sell if there is real demand.

A clean-looking product with no demand is still a bad idea.

That does not mean the product model is bad. It just means it is less forgiving if you guess wrong. If money is urgent, building a product before you understand what people actually want can waste precious time.

3. The Hybrid Model: Service First, Product Later

This is often the smartest long-term option.

You start with a service to bring in cash and learn what people need. Then you turn what you learn into a product later.

Let's say you help five job seekers improve their resumes. You start noticing the same problems over and over. Their summaries are weak. Their bullet points are vague. Their cover letters all sound flat. Now you are no longer guessing what to build. You can create a resume toolkit, a cover letter guide, or an interview answer pack based on real patterns.

Or maybe you help local businesses with captions and review responses. After doing this for a few clients, you realise they all struggle with the same thing: staying consistent. Now you can create a caption bank, a monthly content calendar, or a review-response template pack.

That is why the hybrid model works so well. The service teaches you what the product should be.

Instead of building in the dark, you build from evidence.

Why One Path Beats Five Half-Started Ideas

Because momentum matters more than variety.

Every time you switch directions, you reset the clock.

You lose:

- clarity
- confidence
- progress

- practice
- pattern recognition

Sticking with one model long enough helps you get sharper. Your message improves. Your offer becomes easier to explain. You start hearing the same objections, seeing the same problems, and noticing what people respond to.

That is where skill comes from.

Not from reading more. From repeating the right kind of work.

Imagine two beginners.

The first spends 30 days jumping between ideas. One day, they are making prompt packs. The next day, they are researching affiliate marketing. Then they decide to sell templates. Then they consider cold emailing local businesses, but feel unsure and stop.

The second spends 30 days doing one thing: helping job seekers rewrite resumes and cover letters using AI to speed up the process.

Who is more likely to make money?

Almost always, the second person.

Not because the idea is more glamorous. Because they gave one path enough time to breathe.

The Fast Cash vs. Long-Term Asset Decision

You need to answer one question honestly:

Do I need money soon, or can I afford to build slowly?

Do not answer with what sounds ambitious. Answer with what is true.

If your bills are pressing, your savings are low, or you simply need proof that this can work, choose the path that gets you closer to cash. That is usually a service.

If you are not under immediate pressure and you enjoy building systems, templates, or resources, a simple product can make sense. But it still needs validation.

If you want both, do them in the right order:

1. start with a service
2. learn the demand
3. Turn repeated work into a product.

That order removes a lot of pain.

Many people try to do it backwards. They build a product first because it sounds efficient, then wonder why no one buys. They did not fail because the products do not work. They failed because they tried to skip the learning stage.

Services can feel less glamorous. They are often more useful.

How to Choose Based on Personality, Time, and Urgency

This part matters. A path can look good on paper and still be wrong for you.

Choose based on how you actually work, not how you wish you worked.

If you are shy, choose behind-the-scenes services.

Not everyone wants to be visible online. Not everyone wants to make videos, sell in public, or post their face every day.

You do not have to.

There is plenty of demand for quiet, useful work done behind the scenes.

Examples:

- summarizing research
- organizing notes
- formatting documents
- cleaning up transcripts
- drafting emails
- repurposing content
- helping with admin tasks

If you are thoughtful, reliable, and comfortable helping from the background, this can be a strong fit.

Quiet people often think they are at a disadvantage online. They are not. They just need a model that does not depend on performance.

If you are a strong writer, choose messaging or content help

If words come naturally to you, even a little, that is an asset.

Many people know what they do but struggle to explain it clearly. Their website sounds generic. Their social posts are clumsy. Their resume undersells them. Their emails are too long or too vague.

This is where writing-based offers shine.

Examples:

- resume rewrites
- cover letters
- LinkedIn summaries
- website copy clean-up
- social captions
- email sequences
- product descriptions
- short-form content repurposing

AI can help you brainstorm, draft, shorten, reframe, and improve structure. But the real value is still your judgment. Your ability to make the message clearer, sharper, and more useful.

That is what people pay for.

If you are organised, choose research, summarising, or admin support

Some people have a quiet superpower: they can take chaos and turn it into order.

That skill is valuable.

Business owners, freelancers, coaches, and busy professionals are drowning in loose notes, unread links, half-finished documents, voice memos, meeting notes, and scattered ideas.

If you can step into that mess and produce clarity, you have an offer.

Examples:

- research summaries
- competitor snapshots
- meeting-note clean-ups
- FAQ documents
- inbox draft support
- process documents
- summary reports from long articles, videos, or transcripts

This kind of work is not flashy. It is deeply useful.

Useful gets paid.

If you need money urgently, choose local business offers or job-seeker services.

When income is urgent, go toward pain that people already understand.

Two markets stand out:

Local businesses

They need help showing up online, replying professionally, staying visible, and communicating clearly.

Simple offers include:

- ready-to-post captions

- review response drafts

- basic promo copy

- FAQ page writing

- email drafts

- Google Business Profile content ideas

Job seeker

They are often stressed, discouraged, and willing to pay for help that makes them feel more confident.

Simple offers include:

- resume rewrites

- cover letters

- LinkedIn profile improvements

- Interview prep documents

- Job application support

These markets are good because the value is easy to explain.

A restaurant owner understands, "I can help you stay active online without spending hours on content."

A job seeker understands, "I can help you present yourself better and apply with more confidence."

That clarity matters.

Matching Offers to Real-World Demand

A lot of beginners start with the wrong question.

They ask, "What could I sell?"

A better question is, "What problem is already bothering people enough that they want help?"

The market does not pay for vague creativity. It pays for relief.

People pay faster when the problem is:

- frustrating
- repetitive
- time-consuming
- embarrassing
- tied to money
- tied to opportunity
- mentally draining

That is why good beginner offers usually sit around communication, organisation, visibility, hiring, or saving time.

Here is the difference between a weak offer and a strong one.

Weak:

"I sell AI prompt packs."

Stronger:

"I help job seekers turn messy work history into a professional resume and cover letter."

Weak:

"I do AI services for businesses."

Stronger:

"I create 15 ready-to-post captions and 10 review responses for local businesses that struggle to stay active online."

Weak:

"I help with research."

Stronger:

"I turn scattered articles, notes, and links into a one-page summary a busy business owner can actually use."

The stronger version wins because it is specific. You can picture it. You can see the value. You can imagine paying for it.

That is what you want.

How to Validate an Idea without Spending Money

You do not need a paid ad budget. You do not need branding. You do not need to "launch."

You need signs that the problem is real.

Here is how to find them for free.

1. Look for repeated pain

Search for places where people talk honestly:

- Reddit
- Facebook groups
- LinkedIn posts

- Job boards
- Online communities
- Comments under relevant videos or posts

Look for phrases like:

- "This takes forever"
- "I have no idea how to do this"
- "I'm overwhelmed"
- "I hate writing these"
- "Can someone help me with this?"
- "I keep putting this off"

Repeated pain is a clue. Repeated pain from the same type of person is an opportunity.

2. See whether people already pay for similar help

Look at marketplaces, service listings, or freelancers already offering something similar.

You are not doing this to copy them. You are checking whether the market already understands the value.

Ask:

- Are people paying for this kind of help?
- How is the offer described?
- What outcome is being promised?
- Can I make this simpler or clearer?

If others are already selling related help, that is usually a good sign.

3. Talk to real people, not supportive friends

Friends will often tell you your idea sounds great. They are trying to be kind. Kindness is not validation.

Instead, ask someone in the target market:

- What part of this is most frustrating for you?
- What usually slows you down?
- What have you tried already?
- What would make this easier?
- If someone solved this for you, what would matter most?

You are not fishing for compliments. You are listening for pain.

4. Offer a small version first

Do not build the big version before testing the small version.

If your idea is resume help, offer one resume rewrite.
If your idea is social media help, offer five captions.
If your idea is research support, offer one summary.
If your idea is content repurposing, offer one post turned into three short pieces.

Small tests save time. They also get your feedback faster.

5. Pay attention to action, not interest

The strongest sign is not "That sounds cool."

It is:

- "How much?"

- "Can you do this for me?"
- "I need that."
- "When can you start?"

That is the moment an idea becomes a real offer.

The One-Offer Rule for the First 30 Days

For your first month, follow one rule:

One niche. One problem. One offer. One kind of person.

This rule will save you from yourself.

In the beginning, your brain will want to add things. More services. More options. More niches. More flexibility.

Do not do it.

The goal is not to look impressive. The goal is to make it easy for people to understand what you do.

Here is what that can look like.

Example one:

- niche: job seekers
- Problem: weak applications
- offer: resume and cover letter rewrite
- person: recent graduates or career changers

Example two:

- niche: local businesses

- Problem: inconsistent online presence

- offer: monthly caption pack plus review responses

- person: salon owners, restaurant owners, or independent service providers

Example three:

- niche: coaches

- problem: too much content, not enough time

- offer: turn one long video into short posts

- person: solo coaches who post on LinkedIn or Instagram

When you narrow things down, you become easier to trust.

People do not buy when they are confused. They buy when the offer feels relevant.

Step-by-Step Action Plan

Now let's make this practical.

You are going to choose your path today.

Step 1: Choose your main goal for the next 30 days

Pick the most true sentence:

- I need money fast.

- I want to build something I can sell more than once.

- I want both, but income comes first.

Your answer points you here:

- **Money fast** = service model

- **Sell more than once** = product model
- **Both, but income first** = hybrid model

No overthinking. Pick the one that matches your actual situation.

Step 2: Choose the kind of work that fits you best

Which one sounds most natural?

- I am better at writing than speaking.
- I am good at organising messy information.
- I prefer working behind the scenes.
- I need something I can offer quickly.
- I like building templates, guides, or resources.

This helps you narrow the offer type.

For example:

- writing strength -> messaging, captions, resumes, emails
- organised mind -> research, summaries, admin support
- shy personality -> behind-the-scenes services
- urgent income -> local businesses or job seekers
- builder mind-set -> simple product, but validate first

Step 3: Pick one market

Choose one group you can understand and reach.

Good beginner markets:

- job seekers
- local businesses

- freelancers

- coaches

- creators

- students

- busy professionals

- real estate agents

- service providers

Do not choose based on what sounds trendy. Choose based on where the pain feels obvious.

Step 4: Pick one problem inside that market

Keep it tight.

Examples:

- job seekers -> weak resumes

- local businesses -> no time for social media

- Freelancers -> poor client communication

- coaches -> content takes too long

- busy professionals -> too much information, no clear summary

Narrow wins.

Step 5: Turn the problem into one offer

Use this sentence:

I help [type of person] solve [specific problem] by providing [simple offer].

Examples:

- I help job seekers improve weak applications by rewriting their resumes and cover letters.
- I help local business owners stay visible online by creating ready-to-post captions and review responses.
- I help busy founders save time by turning messy notes into clear summaries and action documents.

That sentence becomes the backbone of your offer.

Step 6: Validate it with five real-world checks

Do five quick checks today:

1. Find two places online where people in that market talk about the problem.
2. Read what language they use.
3. Find one person already offering similar help.
4. Write down what result they promise.
5. Message one real person or identify one person you could help first.

Do not get lost in research. This should take less than an hour.

Step 7: Create a starter offer

Make it small enough that somebody can say yes without a long decision.

Examples:

- **Resume Starter Pack**: one resume rewrite + one cover letter draft
- **Visibility Starter Pack**: 15 social captions + 10 review responses
- **Research Starter Pack**: one summary document from notes, links, or transcripts
- **Content Repurpose Pack**: one video turned into five short posts

Your first offer does not need to be huge. It needs to be clear.

Step 8: Commit for 30 days

Write this down somewhere visible:

For the next 30 days, I will focus on one niche, one problem, one offer, and one type of person.

This matters because your biggest enemy is not a lack of opportunity.

It is the urge to switch too soon.

Common Mistakes to Avoid

1. Choosing what sounds impressive instead of what sells

Fancy ideas attract beginners. Simple offers get bought.

Nobody cares how clever your model is if they do not understand the value.

2. Being too broad

If your offer is for "business owners" or "anyone who needs help," it is too wide.

The more specific you are, the easier it is for people to recognise themselves in the offer.

3. Building before validating

Do not spend a week making templates, pages, or designs before checking whether the problem is real.

Validation first. Packaging second.

4. Switching because you feel uncertain

Uncertainty is part of the process. It does not automatically mean you chose wrong.

Sometimes the discomfort you feel is not a sign to pivot. It is a sign to keep going.

5. Ignoring your financial reality

If you need money now, stop trying to act like a start-up founder building long-term assets from day one.

Choose the path that fits your pressure, not your ego.

6. Making the offer vague

"AI help for brands" is vague.

"10 captions and 10 review responses for local salons" is clear.

Clarity gets replies.

7. Mistaking polite interest for demand

"Nice idea" does not pay your bills.

You want signs of real need:

- questions about price
- questions about timing
- questions about how it works
- actual requests for help

That is what counts.

Quick Win Task

Do this before you finish today?

Open your notes app and fill in these four lines.

My niche is:
Choose one group.

The problem I solve is:
Choose one pain point they already feel.

My offer is:
Write one simple service or product.

The first person I can help is:
Write one real name. Not a vague audience. One actual person.

Now turn it into this sentence:

I help [who] solve [problem] with [offer].

Here are a few examples:

- I help recent graduates improve weak job applications with resume and cover letter rewrites.
- I help local salon owners stay consistent online with ready-made captions and review responses.
- I help busy consultants reduce information overload with clean research summaries.

That is your decision on paper.

And that matters more than you think.

Because once you can say clearly what you do, you stop sounding unsure. You stop sounding like you are "trying things." You start sounding like somebody who solves a specific problem.

That shift is powerful.

You do not need another week of thinking.

You need a choice.

Not a perfect one. A useful one.

This is where many people lose months. They keep trying to reduce all risk before they begin. But there is no risk-free path. There is only the path you commit to long enough to learn from.

That is how your first $1,000 happens.

Not through endless planning.
Not through chasing every trend.
Not through building five half-finished projects.

It happens when you choose one clear problem, one clear offer, and one real person to help.

That is all this chapter is asking you to do.

Choose your path.
Keep it simple.
Stick with it for 30 days.
Let action teach you what thinking never will.

Your first income usually begins with a quiet decision no one else sees.

Make that decision now.

Chapter 4: You're AI Starter Stack: Free Tools That Actually Help

When you do not have much money, every decision feels heavier than it should.

You do not just ask, "Which tool should I use?"
You ask, "What if I choose the wrong one?"
"What if I waste time?"
"What if I sign up for a bunch of stuff and still do not make a dollar?"

That fear is real. Especially when you are already under pressure.

Maybe you have watched people online show off complicated systems with dashboards, automations, premium software, and fifteen tabs open at once. Maybe part of you assumed that is what "serious" people do.

It is not.

In the beginning, too many tools do not make you more professional. They make you slower, more scattered, and more overwhelmed.

The truth is, your first $1,000 will probably come from a very small stack of simple tools used well. Not from some genius setup. Not from expensive subscriptions. Not from turning your laptop into a control centre.

You need a handful of tools that help you think clearly, create faster, stay organised, and actually send work out into the world.

That is what this chapter is about.

Not the coolest tools.
Not the newest tools.
The ones that actually help.

Reality Check

A lot of beginners get stuck here without realising it.

They think they are building momentum, but what they are really doing is hiding in setup.

They sign up for one tool, then another. They watch comparison videos. They save "best AI tools for 2026" posts. They test things they do not need. By the end of the week, they have done a lot of clicking and have almost no earnings.

It feels productive because it looks like progress.

But it is not.

No client has ever paid someone because their tool stack looked impressive.

People pay for outcomes.

They pay because you helped them write something faster, package something better, organise something messy, turn rough ideas into usable content, or make their life a little easier.

That is the real job.

So let's clear something up right now: you do not need to become a "tool person." You do not need to master a complex tech ecosystem. You do not need to understand every feature.

You need a few beginner-friendly tools that help you do real work.

That is all.

And there is actually a big advantage in keeping things simple early on. A smaller stack forces you to focus on the part that matters most: using the tools to solve problems.

Not collecting them.

Solution Breakdown

The beginner rule: use fewer tools, better

This is the rule I wish more beginners heard on day one:

Use fewer tools, but use them deeply.

That one rule can save you months of distraction.

You do not need three AI writers. You do not need two design platforms. You do not need a complicated project management system when you do not even have your first client yet.

One good tool per job is enough.

One writing tool.

One design tool.

One place to store your work.

One place to track leads.

One way to communicate.

Simple wins because simple gets repeated.

And repeated actions are what build income.

Think about someone trying to get in shape. The person who buys expensive gear, reads twelve workout plans, and never trains will lose to the person who does basic exercises four times a week. Business works the same way. Consistency beats complexity.

Your goal is not to build the perfect stack. Your goal is to build a stack you will actually use when you are tired, busy, or doubting yourself.

That is the stack that makes money.

The essential categories

You only need tools that cover a few basic jobs:

- Writing and brainstorming
- Design
- Documents and workflow
- Voice and transcription
- Research and organization
- Outreach and communication

That is it.

If your tools can help you do those things, you have enough to start.

Now let's make each one practical.

Writing and brainstorming tools

Your main tool here is **ChatGPT or a similar AI assistant**.

For a beginner, this is one of the most useful tools you can have because it helps you move past blank-page paralysis. It gives you a place to start.

Use it for:

- brainstorming offer ideas
- drafting social posts
- writing first-pass emails
- cleaning up rough notes
- turning bullet points into usable copy
- creating outlines, captions, checklists, and simple content drafts

What it is good at is speed.

What it is not good at is judgment.

That part is still yours.

This matters because beginners usually make one of two mistakes. They either think, "I'm not smart enough to use AI," or they think, "AI will do all of this for me." Neither is true.

You do not need to be technical. You just need to be clear.

And AI will not build your income for you. It will help you move faster once you know what problem you are solving.

Here is a simple example.

Let's say you want to offer content help to local businesses. A bakery, a dog groomer, a personal trainer, a cleaning service. They know they should post more online, but they are busy and inconsistent.

You could use ChatGPT to:

- generate 15 post ideas for their business
- Turn those ideas into captions.
- Rewrite the captions to sound more local and human, and create a one-page monthly content plan.

That is useful work. Work someone might pay for.

Notice what happened there: the AI did not create the business. It helped you deliver the service.

That is the mind-set.

A few simple prompts can go a long way:

- "Give me 10 friendly Instagram post ideas for a local bakery trying to attract more repeat customers."
- "Turn these messy notes into a one-page content plan for a dog grooming business."
- "Rewrite this message so it sounds warm, natural, and not salesy."

- "Create a simple checklist a small business owner can use to improve their social media profile."

You do not need perfect prompts. You need useful ones.

Design tools

Your main design tool is **Canva**.

Canva is one of the best beginner tools because it helps ordinary people make clean, usable visuals without needing professional design skills.

That matters more than you think.

Most people do not expect cinematic design. They just want things to look clear, trustworthy, and put together.

You can use Canva for:

- simple PDFs
- lead magnets
- social media graphics
- quote posts
- checklists
- mini-guides
- simple proposals
- service one-pagers
- carousel posts

What Canva does well is packaging.

It helps take rough ideas and present them in a way that feels more valuable.

And presentation matters. Two people can give the same advice, but the one who packages it clearly often gets taken more seriously.

Still, let's be honest about what Canva cannot do. It cannot make weak ideas strong. It cannot fix bad messaging. It cannot turn lazy work into valuable work.

A pretty PDF with useless content is still useless.

So, use Canva for what it is: a way to make useful work easier to consume.

Here is a real beginner scenario:
You offer a local café ten content ideas for the month. You could paste them into a plain document. That works. But if you package them into a clean one-page PDF in Canva, suddenly it feels more real. More polished. More deliverable.

That small shift can make a beginner offer feel much more credible.

Document and workflow tools

Your bread-and-butter tools here are **Google Docs** and **Google Sheets**.

These are not exciting tools.

That is exactly why they matter.

They are reliable. They are easy to use. They are easy to share. And they keep your work from disappearing into chaos.

Use Google Docs for:

- saving prompts
- writing deliverables
- drafting outreach
- storing client notes
- creating templates
- writing product content
- keeping service scripts and sample drafts

Use Google Sheets for:

- tracking leads
- tracking outreach
- tracking follow-ups
- tracking payments
- organising offer ideas
- managing simple content calendars

A lot of beginners think their problem is a lack of talent. Sometimes the problem is simpler than that: they are disorganised.

Their ideas are in one app. Their draft is in another. Their client notes are buried in messages. Their outreach list is nowhere. Every task takes twice as long because they are always looking for something.

That kind of mess drains energy fast.

When your system is clean, your work feels lighter. You know where things go. You know what comes next. You stop restarting every day.

That is not a small benefit. It is one of the things that makes consistency possible.

Writing Polish tools

Use **Grammarly or built-in writing tools** to clean up your work before you send it.

This is not about sounding fancy. It is about sounding careful.

People make trust decisions very quickly. Sloppy writing signals sloppiness everywhere else, even if that is not fair.

Use writing polish tools for:

- grammar checks
- clearer sentence structure
- fixing awkward wording
- improving readability
- cleaning up outreach messages and deliverables

What they do not do is create strong thinking for you.

They can polish weak writing, but they cannot give weak ideas more value. They are a finishing step, not a strategy.

Still, that finishing step matters.

If you are sending a pitch, a short PDF, a client sample, or a follow-up email, taking five extra minutes to clean it up can make a real difference in how professional you feel and how seriously the other person takes you.

Research and organisation tools

Your main option here is **Notion or a simple notes app**.

It really can be that basic.

You do not need a beautiful digital headquarters. You need one place to keep useful things.

Use it for:

- prompt ideas
- niche research
- offer ideas
- saved examples
- objections you hear from prospects
- content inspiration
- Lessons from what worked and what flopped

This becomes your working notebook.

Over time, this is where your business brain starts to live.

But there is a trap here.

Organisation tools are excellent at making procrastination look respectable.

A beginner can spend hours building pages, labels, dashboards, and systems instead of actually sending one offer into the world. It feels like business building, but often it is fear wearing nicer clothes.

So keep this part simple.

If Notion helps you stay organised, great. Use it. If your phone's notes app is faster and easier, use that. There is no prize for having the most sophisticated setup.

The best system is the one you open and use.

Voice and transcription tools

Free transcription tools can be incredibly useful, especially if you talk more easily than you write.

A lot of people do.

Sometimes your best ideas show up when you are walking, driving, cooking, or lying awake worrying about money. In those moments, speaking is easier than trying to type a polished paragraph.

Use transcription tools for:

- turning voice notes into text
- pulling text from short videos
- drafting content from spoken ideas
- repurposing audio into captions, emails, or posts
- helping clients turn rough voice notes into usable content

This can be helpful for your own workflow, but it can also become part of your offer.

For example, imagine a busy coach sends you three voice notes with their content ideas for the week. You transcribe them, organise them, clean them up with AI, and turn them into five social posts and one email draft.

That is not magic. That is service.

The transcription tool gives you raw material. Your job is to shape it into something useful.

Email and messaging apps for outreach

This category is not glamorous, but it is the one most connected to getting paid.

Use **email, Instagram DMs, LinkedIn, Facebook messages, WhatsApp, or whatever platform makes sense for your audience**.

These tools matter because no offer earns money in silence.

You can create the best sample in the world, but if nobody sees it, it does not matter.

Use these apps for:

- outreach
- follow-ups
- conversations
- checking needs
- sending samples
- delivering small pieces of work
- building simple client relationships

This is where a lot of beginners break the chain. They create, organise, and polish, but they never send.

They keep "getting ready."

Please hear this clearly: your business does not start when your tools are set up. It starts when you begin making contact.

That can be uncomfortable. I know. Reaching out feels vulnerable. Especially when you are new. Especially when you are afraid of sounding awkward or being ignored.

But awkward action beats polished hesitation every single time.

What each tool is good for—and what it is not

Let's make this as clear as possible.

ChatGPT or a similar AI assistant

Good for: idea generation, drafting, rewriting, outlining, brainstorming, speeding up first drafts
Not good for: replacing your judgment, guaranteeing quality without editing, and building trust for you.

Canva

Good for: simple visuals, lead magnets, PDFs, social graphics, checklists, and clean presentation.
Not good for: advanced design work, fixing weak ideas, making bad offers feel valuable.

Google Docs

Good for: writing, storing templates, draft creation, client notes, and deliverables.

Not good for: managing complex workflows by itself

Google Sheets

Good for: lead tracking, follow-ups, payments, outreach lists, and basic organisation.

Not good for: writing polished content or replacing a clear process

Grammarly or built-in writing tools

Good for: polishing, grammar, tightening language, catching errors.

Not good for: creating original thinking or strategy

Notion or a notes app

Good for: saving ideas, prompts, examples, research, and lessons learned.

Not good for: becoming another project that keeps you from real work

Free transcription tools

Good for: converting speech to text, repurposing audio, and helping you create faster.

Not good for: delivering final content without clean-up

Email and messaging apps

Good for: outreach, relationship-building, follow-up, and delivery.

Not good for: helping you if you keep avoiding the send button

How to use free plans wisely

When money is tight, free plans are not a disadvantage. They are protection.

They stop you from paying for excitement.

That matters because beginner energy is expensive when it is unmanaged. You get inspired, sign up for three premium trials, tell yourself you are "investing in the business," and then one week later, you are overwhelmed, discouraged, and being billed for tools you barely touched.

Do not do that to yourself.

Use free plans like this:

1. Stay free until the free version becomes a real problem

Not an imaginary problem. A real one.

Upgrade only when:

- You are using the tool often
- The limits are slowing down paid work
- The upgrade would clearly save time
- The tool is already part of your normal workflow

2. Let revenue pay for upgrades

This is a healthier rule than "buy now and hope."

Instead of saying, "Maybe this premium plan will help me finally make money," say, "This tool is already helping me work, and now I can justify improving it."

That simple mind-set shift will protect you from a lot of unnecessary spending.

3. Watch your actual usage

A tool sounds useful, and a tool is useful are two different things.

Ask yourself:

- Did I use this last week?
- Did it help me create, sell, or deliver something?
- Would my workflow noticeably suffer without it?

If not, you probably do not need to pay for it.

4. Ignore feature envy

Beginners often get pulled toward advanced features because experienced creators talk about them.

But at your stage, the feature that matters most is repeatability.

Can you use the tool consistently? Can you get useful output from it without stress? Can it help you complete work this week?

That is what matters.

Beginner-friendly tools that make sense right now

Here is a practical starter stack for most beginners:

- **ChatGPT or a similar AI assistant** for writing, brainstorming, and rough drafts
- **Canva** for simple visuals, PDFs, and social graphics
- **Google Docs** for writing and delivery
- **Google Sheets** for tracking leads and progress
- **Grammarly or built-in writing help** for polishing
- **Notion or a notes app** for storing prompts, ideas, and examples
- **A free transcription tool** for voice-to-text and repurposing
- **Email and messaging apps** for outreach

That is enough.

Enough to build a service. Enough to create a simple digital product. Enough to contact people. Enough to organise your work. Enough to start.

You do not need more than that right now.

Practical setup

Create a "Money Folder"

This sounds small. It is not.

Create one folder on your laptop, desktop, or cloud storage called:

Money Folder

Inside it, create these subfolders:

- Offers

- Outreach
- Samples
- Client Work
- Prompts
- Templates
- Payments
- Ideas

This is one of those quiet habits that changes everything.

Because when your work lives in random places, every task feels heavier. You waste time finding files, redoing work, searching for drafts, and wondering where you saved that one message that actually sounded good.

A clean folder does something powerful: it reduces friction.

And when you are trying to build momentum, friction is the enemy.

Save prompts, templates, and examples in one place

Anything useful should be saved the moment you create it.

A good outreach message? Save it.
A prompt that gave you solid results? Save it.
A clean Canva layout? Save it as a template.
A client draft structure that worked well? Save it.

Do not trust yourself to remember it later.

You are not just doing one-off tasks. You are building a library.

That library becomes speed.

And speed matters because the more quickly you can move from idea to deliverable, the easier it becomes to stay consistent.

Build a repeatable workflow.

Your life gets easier when you stop creating from scratch every time.

Let's say your first simple offer is content help for local businesses. A repeatable workflow might look like this:

1. Use Google Sheets to list 20 local businesses
2. Use ChatGPT to draft a warm outreach message
3. Send those messages by email or DM
4. Save responses and notes in Google Docs
5. Use ChatGPT to generate ideas based on the business type
6. Clean and package the ideas in Canva
7. Polish the final wording with Grammarly
8. Deliver it as a Google Doc or PDF
9. Save the finished version inside your Samples folder
10. Track follow-up and payment in Sheets

That is a simple business system.

Not fancy. Not complicated. But real.

And real beats impressive every time.

Step-by-Step Action Plan

Here is what to do today.

Step 1: Pick your stack

Choose one tool for each job:

- one writing tool
- one design tool
- one note or organisation tool
- one document tool
- one tracking tool
- one communication channel

Do not give yourself six options. Pick one.

Step 2: Build your Money Folder

Create the folder and the subfolders.

This should take a few minutes, not an hour.

Step 3: Create your working documents

Open Google Docs and create:

- Saved Prompts
- Outreach Scripts
- Offer Ideas

Open Google Sheets and create:

- Lead Tracker
- Follow-Up Tracker
- Income Tracker

Keep them simple. Messy but usable beats beautiful but unfinished.

Step 4: Save five prompts you can reuse

Start with prompts that help you create faster.

For example:

- "Write a warm outreach message offering help with social media content for a local business."
- "Give me 10 content ideas for a [type of business] trying to attract local customers."
- "Turn these notes into a simple one-page PDF outline."
- "Rewrite this so it sounds more natural and less pushy."
- "Summarise these ideas into a checklist for beginners."

Step 5: Make one Canva template

Create one reusable asset:

- a one-page offer sheet
- a simple content plan
- a checklist
- a mini-guide
- a social post template

This is not about perfection. It is about giving yourself something reusable.

Step 6: Choose one outreach channel

Pick the channel you are most likely to use consistently.

Not the trendiest one. The most realistic one.

If email feels easiest, use email. If Instagram makes more sense for your niche, use Instagram. If you are targeting professionals, maybe LinkedIn works better.

Start where action is most likely.

Step 7: Run one full test

Do not stop at setup. Test the system.

Pick one niche.
Create one simple offer.
Draft one outreach message.
Make one sample.
Save it all.

You do not need to be perfect. You need proof that your workflow works.

That proof builds confidence faster than motivational speeches ever will.

Common Mistakes to Avoid

Signing up for too many tools

This is the biggest one.

Too many tools create too many decisions. Too many decisions create hesitation. Hesitation turns into delay. Delay turns into self-doubt.

Keep it lean.

Paying for the premium too early

Do not buy subscriptions to feel like you are "taking this seriously."

Serious people do the work first.

Let the work earn the upgrade.

Letting tools become a distraction

This happens more than people admit.

You tell yourself you are working, but the whole day disappears into:

- testing platforms
- reorganizing folders
- comparing features
- watching tutorials
- tweaking templates

Meanwhile, no outreach was sent. No offer was made. No sample was finished.

Be careful here. Tool research can become a very socially acceptable form of avoidance.

Expecting the tools to carry you

No tool can choose your niche, face rejection, follow up with prospects, or build trust in your place.

Tools support action. They do not replace it.

Building systems before proving demand

Do not spend a week creating the perfect setup for a service nobody has said yes to yet.

Find out whether people want the offer first. Improve the system after that.

Confusing polished work with useful work

A clean design helps. Good grammar helps. Nice structure helps.

But usefulness comes first.

Always ask, "Does this actually help someone solve a small problem?"

That question will save you from making attractive but empty work.

Quick Win Task

Do this before you leave this chapter.

Set a timer for 30 minutes and complete the following:

- Create your Money Folder
- Choose your core tools
- Open one Google Doc called Saved Prompts
- Open one Google Sheet called Lead Tracker
- Save five useful prompts
- Make one simple Canva template
- Choose one outreach channel

That is enough for today.

You do not need a full business dashboard by tonight. You need a functional starting point.

And once you have that, starting tomorrow gets easier.

You are not trying to become a software expert.

You are trying to become useful.

That is a much simpler goal, and a much more profitable one.

So do not let the internet convince you that you need a giant stack, premium subscriptions, or some elaborate system before you can begin. Most of that noise is just another form of procrastination dressed up as ambition.

Keep your tools basic.
Keep your workflow clear.
Keep your attention on work that can be created, sent, and paid for.

That is how this starts.

Not with the perfect setup.
With a usable one.

Not with confidence.
With movement.

Not with ten tools.
With the right few.

Your first $1,000 is much more likely to come from simple tools used consistently than from complicated tools used occasionally.

So build your stack like someone who needs results, not like someone trying to look impressive online.

Because right now, simple is not a weakness.

Simple is your edge.

Chapter 5: Learn Just Enough AI to Get Paid

One of the biggest lies keeping people stuck right now is this:

"I need to really understand AI before I can make money with it."

No, you do not.

You do not need to master AI.
You do not need to speak in technical language.
You do not need to spend weeks watching tutorials until your brain feels full and your bank account still looks the same.

You need one thing:

You need to know how to use AI well enough to produce work that helps someone.

That is it.

This matters because when money is tight, "learning for months" sounds responsible, but it often becomes a form of hiding. It feels productive. It sounds smart. But in reality, it delays the only thing that builds real confidence: doing useful work in the real world.

Maybe you have already felt this tension.

You open an AI tool. You type something in. The answer comes back too broad, too weird, too polished, or just plain useless. Then that old fear shows up again:

"See? I knew this wasn't for me."

"I'm not technical."

"I don't know how to use this properly."

"Other people get it. I don't."

That fear is understandable. But it is also misleading.

Because the people making money with AI at the beginner level are usually not the most technical. They are the most practical.

They learn how to get a decent result.
Then they improve it.
Then they turn that result into something another person can use.

That is the game.

A local business owner does not care whether you understand advanced AI concepts.
They care whether you can help them write better posts, organise messy ideas, improve product descriptions, or turn a long transcript into usable content.

A job seeker does not care whether you can explain how large language models work.
They care whether you can turn their rough notes into a résumé summary that sounds clear, credible, and professional.

The market is not paying beginners for technical brilliance.

It is paying for useful outcomes.

And that should take a lot of pressure off your shoulders.

This chapter will show you the minimum level of AI skill you actually need to start delivering value. Not theory. Not hype. Not "10X your life with automation" nonsense.

Just the simple, real-world skill of using AI as a tool to create something worth paying for.

Reality Check

Let's be honest, so you do not build false confidence.

AI can help you move faster. It can help you brainstorm, draft, rewrite, summarise, organise, simplify, and repurpose content. In the hands of a beginner, that is already powerful.

But AI is not a magic wand.

It gets things wrong.
It makes things up.
It often sounds polished in a way that feels fake.
It repeats itself.
It fills blank spaces with generic fluff.
And if you let it do all the thinking, your work will sound like everyone else's.

That is why the real skill is not "using AI."

The real skill is **guiding AI well enough to get a strong draft, then using your own judgment to make it better.**

That is much easier than becoming an expert.

But it still requires effort.

Here is the good news: the effort is manageable.

You do not need to know everything AI can do.
You do not need to use twenty tools.
You do not need to become "the AI person."

You need a repeatable process.

Think of AI like a fast but careless assistant.

If you hand that assistant a vague instruction, you will get vague work.
If you fail to explain the goal, you will get confused output.
If you copy and paste the first draft without reading it, you will eventually embarrass yourself.

But if you give clear direction, ask for better options, refine the result, and check the final version like a responsible adult, AI becomes incredibly useful.

That is the level you are aiming for.

Not mastery.
Not perfection.
Useful output.

And useful output is enough to get paid.

Solution Breakdown

You do not need mastery—you need usable output

This is the mind-set shift that makes everything simpler.

Most beginners think the goal is to "get good at AI."
That sounds impressive, but it is too vague to help you.

A better goal is this:

Can I use AI to create something clear, helpful, and usable for another person?

That question leads to income.
Because clients do not buy your knowledge of AI.
They buy the result.

They buy:

- a better résumé summary
- 30 social media ideas
- cleaner product descriptions
- a simple blog draft
- short posts from a long transcript
- a polished email sequence
- a clearer offer page

They are paying for saved time, improved communication, and less mental effort on their side.

That means your job is not to impress people with AI.
Your job is to quietly use it to solve problems faster.

Once you understand that, the whole thing becomes less intimidating.

You are not trying to become the smartest person in the room. You are trying to be the most useful.

That is a much more reachable target.

The beginner's AI workflow

If you remember nothing else from this chapter, remember this four-step workflow:

1. Give context

Tell AI what the task is, who it is for, and what good looks like.

2. Ask for options

Do not settle for the first answer. Ask for variations, different angles, or several versions.

3. Improve the result

Take the strongest draft and refine it until it sounds clearer, more specific, and more human.

4. Human-check everything

Read it, edit it, verify it, and make sure it actually makes sense.

That is the workflow.

Simple enough to use today.
Strong enough to build a service around.

Let's walk through each part.

1. Give context

This is where most people go wrong.

They type something lazy like:

"Write me an Instagram post."

And then they get a boring answer and assume AI is the problem.

Usually, it is not.

The problem is the instruction.

Imagine asking a human assistant the same thing. They would have questions immediately.

For who?
About what?
What is the goal?
What tone should it have?
Who is the audience?
Should it be short, funny, educational, or persuasive?

AI needs that same direction.

Here is a weak prompt:

"Write a caption for a gym."

Now compare it with this:

Write 5 Instagram captions for a local gym that helps busy adults lose weight in a realistic way. The audience is men and women aged 30–45 who feel intimidated by extreme fitness culture. Make the tone encouraging, simple, and friendly. Each caption should end with a call to action for a free trial session."

That second version is not fancy.
It is just clear.

And clarity changes everything.

When the output is poor, do not immediately conclude that AI is useless.
First, ask whether your instructions were too thin.

A good prompt usually includes:

- the task
- the audience
- the goal
- the tone
- the format
- any limits or special details

That is enough to produce far better work.

2. Ask for options

This one habit alone will improve your results almost overnight.

Do not accept the first answer.

Treat the first answer as a rough draft, not a finished piece.

One of the smartest ways to use AI is to ask for multiple versions so you can compare and choose. This gives you range. It helps you notice what works. It stops you from getting trapped by one mediocre output.

Use prompts like:

- "Give me 3 versions."
- "Show me 5 alternatives."
- "Write 10 headline options."
- "Make one version warmer, one simpler, and one more direct."
- "Give me 3 hooks that would grab attention fast."

This matters because choosing from options feels different from forcing one bad answer into shape.

It is the difference between saying, "I hope this is good enough," and saying, "This one is strongest, so I'll build on that."

That shift gives you more control.
And more control creates better work.

3. Improve the result

This is where average output becomes professional-looking work.

A lot of beginners stop too early. They get something decent, feel relieved, and move on. But that extra round or two of refinement is often where the real value appears.

Once AI gives you a usable draft, your next job is to shape it.

You can say:

- "Make this sound more natural."
- "Simplify the language."

- "Cut the fluff."
- "Make this more persuasive without sounding pushy."
- "Rewrite this for small business owners."
- "Make this warmer and less formal."
- "Turn this into plain English."
- "Remove clichés and generic phrases."

This is where your judgment starts to matter.

Because you are no longer asking AI to create blindly.
You are directing it toward a specific result.

Think of the first draft as uncooked ingredients.
You still have to season the food.

That is why people who know how to refine AI output can earn money from it, while people who only know how to paste prompts into a box usually stay stuck.

4. Human-check everything

This is the part lazy people skip.

Do not skip it.

AI can write something that sounds smooth and still be wrong, awkward, repetitive, or misleading. It can also make things sound more impressive than they really are, which a serious problem is, if you are writing for a client, a résumé, or a business.

Before you deliver anything, ask:

- Is this actually true?

- Does this sound like a real person?

- Is this specific enough?

- Is anything exaggerated?

- Would I be comfortable sending this under my own name?

If the work includes facts, dates, numbers, product details, or claims, verify them.

If it includes a person's background or experience, make sure nothing has been invented.

If it sounds polished but empty, tighten it.

This final review is not a small detail.

It is the difference between using AI responsibly and using it lazily.

And once again, this is where your value lives.

You are not being paid because AI exists.

You are being paid because you can guide it, improve it, and catch what it misses.

How to write prompts that produce useful work

Prompts do not need to be clever

They need to be clear.

A simple structure you can use again and again is this:

Task + Context + Goal + Tone + Format + Constraints

That sounds basic because it is basic. And basic works.

Here is an example for an Etsy seller:

Write 5 product description options for a handmade soy candle sold on Etsy. The audience is women buying cosy gifts for their home or for friends. The goal is to make the candle feel warm, premium, and gift-worthy. Use natural, everyday language. Keep each version under 90 words and avoid generic phrases."

That is a strong beginner prompt.

Here is another for a job seeker:

"Turn these rough notes into 3 résumé summary options for someone applying for customer service roles. Keep the tone professional and honest. Do not exaggerate experience. Make each version 3–4 lines."

That works too.

Notice what is missing:
No complicated prompt formulas.
No dramatic "hack."
No weird technical phrasing.

Just clear instructions.

That is usually enough.

The difference between bad output and bad instructions

This is one of the most important lessons you can learn early.

Sometimes AI gives weak output because the tool is limited. But very often, the output is weak because the instructions were weak.

That is good news, because instructions are something you can improve immediately.

Here is a bad prompt:

"Write product descriptions."

That is too vague to produce anything special.

Here is a better version:

"Write 5 Etsy product descriptions for handmade ceramic mugs. The audience is women aged 25–40 who like calm, cosy home décor and thoughtful gifts. Make the tone warm, simple, and slightly premium. Each description should be 60–80 words and highlight everyday use, craftsmanship, and gift appeal."

Now the AI has direction.
Now it can work with something real.

So the next time you feel disappointed by the output, do not just think, "This tool is bad."
Ask better questions:

- Did I explain who this is for?
- Did I say what the goal is?
- Did I mention tone?
- Did I ask for the format I actually need?

- Did I give enough context to make the answer specific?

That small pause will save you a lot of frustration.

The "draft, edit, verify" system

If you want one simple system to carry into paid work, use this one:

Draft

Get AI to quickly create the first version.

At this stage, you are not chasing perfection.
You are building momentum.

Edit

Shape the draft until it becomes clearer, stronger, and more natural.

This is where you improve tone, fix weak phrasing, remove fluff, simplify language, or make the content more persuasive.

Verify

Check accuracy, usefulness, and fit.

This is where you make sure nothing false, clumsy, or generic slips through.

That is it.

Draft. Edit. Verify.

This system is powerful because it protects you from two common beginner mistakes:
waiting too long to start, and trusting the first draft too much.

You do not need to produce brilliance on command.

You need a process you can trust.

And this one works across almost every beginner-friendly AI service.

When AI is helpful and when human judgment matters more

AI is extremely useful for:

- generating ideas

- creating rough drafts

- rewriting for clarity

- summarizing long text

- turning notes into structured content

- repurposing one piece of content into several smaller assets

- simplifying complicated wording

- brainstorming multiple options fast

But there are areas where human judgment matters much more:

- anything fact-sensitive

- anything emotionally sensitive

- anything involving trust or reputation

- anything requiring strategy

- anything involving health, legal, or financial claims

- anything where brand voice needs to feel very specific and real

For example, AI can absolutely help draft content ideas for a local gym.

But if it starts making irresponsible promises about weight loss, you need to catch that.

AI can help improve a résumé summary.
But if it invents achievements the person never had, you must remove them.

AI can turn a long transcript into short posts.
But you still need to make sure the meaning was not distorted.

Use AI for speed.
Use human judgment for truth, nuance, and trust.

That balance is what keeps your work useful and credible.

How to avoid sounding robotic or generic

This is where many AI-assisted beginners lose the plot.

The content may be technically "fine," but it feels lifeless. It sounds like it was written by someone who has never had a real conversation.

You know the kind of writing I mean.

It is full of phrases like:

- "unlock your potential"
- "take your business to the next level"
- "in today's fast-paced world"
- "high-quality solutions tailored to your needs"

That kind of language sounds polished from far away and empty up close.

Here is how you fix it.

Use real details

Specific writing feels alive.
Generic writing feels disposable.

Instead of:
"Helping businesses grow online"

say:
"Helping local cafés bring in more weekday customers through simple content and better offers"

Instead of:
"This candle is perfect for any occasion"

say:
"A clean-burning soy candle made for slow evenings, quiet mornings, and easy gift-giving"

Details make the reader see something.
And when people can see it, they can feel it.

Ask for plain English

You can tell AI exactly what you want:

- "Use simple everyday language."
- "Make this sound like a real person."
- "Avoid buzzwords."
- "Cut corporate-sounding phrases."
- "Keep it warm, clear, and natural."

- "Write this at a beginner-friendly reading level."

Do not be shy about over-directing here.

Clear instruction is often what saves the output.

Start with something human

AI often works best when it is improving messy real material rather than inventing everything from scratch.

That could be:

- rough notes
- a voice transcript
- an unfinished paragraph
- a messy list of ideas
- product details written badly
- a client's brain dump

Real material has texture.

It has mistakes, yes, but it also has life.

Your job is to use AI to shape that life into something cleaner and more useful.

Read it out loud

This is one of the simplest quality checks in the world.

If it sounds stiff when you say it out loud, it will sound stiff to the reader, too.

Reading aloud helps you catch:

- awkward rhythm
- repetitive phrasing
- fake-sounding enthusiasm
- clunky sentences
- words a normal person would never say

That final human pass matters more than people think.

Simple prompt frameworks

You do not need a giant library of prompts.

You need a few reliable ones you can adapt.

1. "Act as…" prompts for task-specific help

Use these when you want AI to approach the task like a particular professional.

Examples:

"Act as a professional résumé writer. Turn these rough notes into 3 honest, well-written résumé summary options for someone applying for entry-level customer service jobs."

"Act as a social media manager for a local gym. Create 30 simple Instagram content ideas that would appeal to busy adults who want to get healthier without feeling judged."

"Act as an Etsy copywriter. Rewrite these product descriptions so they sound more natural, specific, and gift-worthy."

This helps focus the output without making things complicated.

2. "Give me 3 versions…" prompts for choices

Use this when you want a range.

Examples:

"Give me 3 versions of this caption: one warm, one direct, and one playful."

"Give me 3 résumé summary options with slightly different tones: professional, friendly, and confident."

"Give me 3 product description versions: cosy, elegant, and simple."

Options make your work stronger because they let you choose, combine, and improve.

3. "Improve this for…" prompts for refinement

Use this when you already have something decent and want to make it better.

Examples:

"Improve this for clarity and stronger flow."
"Improve this for conversion, but keep it natural."
"Improve this for beginners who need simple language."
"Improve this so it sounds less robotic and more human."

This is often where the best work happens.

4. "Turn this into a simple version…" prompts for beginner-friendly delivery

Use this when the raw material is too long, too messy, or too dense.

Examples:

"Turn this long transcript into 10 short social posts."

"Turn this product information into a simple Etsy description."

"Turn this rough brain dump into a clean LinkedIn post."

"Turn this into a version a complete beginner could understand."

This type of prompt is especially valuable because many people are overwhelmed not by a lack of ideas, but by messy ideas they cannot organise.

That is where you come in.

Real-World Examples

Turning rough notes into a polished résumé summary

A person sends you this:

"I worked in retail for 3 years. Helped customers, did payments, dealt with complaints sometimes, trained new staff a bit, always on time, want a customer service job."

It is not pretty.
But it is enough.

Here is a prompt you could use:

"Act as a professional résumé writer. Turn these rough notes into 3 résumé summary options for someone applying for customer service roles. Keep them honest, clear, and confident. Do not exaggerate. Make each version 3–4 lines."

Then refine the best one:

"Make version 2 sound more natural and less generic. Keep it professional and easy to read."

A final version might look like this:

"Reliable customer service professional with 3 years of retail experience supporting customers, handling transactions, and helping resolve day-to-day issues calmly and efficiently. Trusted to assist with onboarding new team members and maintain a positive customer experience. Now looking to bring strong communication and problem-solving skills to a dedicated customer service role."

That is a real improvement.
And it is the kind of thing someone will gladly pay for if it helps them apply with more confidence.

Creating 30 social media ideas for a local gym

A local gym owner often knows they should post more, but they are tired, busy, and out of ideas. That is a business problem, not a creativity problem.

You can help with a prompt like this:

"Act as a social media manager for a local gym. Create 30 Instagram content ideas for busy adults aged 30–45 who want to lose weight, feel better, and build healthier habits without extreme workouts or strict diets. Mix educational, motivational, behind-the-scenes, client success, and promotional content."

Then keep going:

"Now turn the best 10 ideas into captions."

"Make the tone more supportive and less intense."

"Remove any ideas that feel overused."

"Add simple calls to action."

Now you have a useful deliverable.

You are not selling "AI content."

You are selling relief to a business owner who no longer has to sit there wondering what to post on Tuesday morning.

That is the real value.

Rewriting product descriptions for an Etsy seller

Many Etsy sellers are talented makers and weak writers. That is not criticism. It is just reality. They put care into the product and rush the listing.

A weak description might say:

"Beautiful handmade candle. Great gift. Made with soy wax. Smells amazing."

It is not wrong.

It is just flat.

Here is a better prompt:

"Act as an Etsy copywriter. Rewrite this candle description for buyers looking for cosy home gifts. Make it feel warm, natural, and slightly premium. Mention handmade soy wax, clean burn, and gift appeal. Keep it under 100 words."

Then refine:

"Give me 3 versions: cosy, simple, and elegant."

"Make the cosy version less cliché."

"Use more sensory detail without overdoing it."

This is practical, easy-to-deliver work.
And for the right seller, it directly supports sales.

Converting a long podcast transcript into short posts

This is one of the easiest beginner services to offer because so many creators are sitting on long-form content they never fully use.

A podcast episode becomes a transcript.
The transcript gets ignored.
You turn it into smaller content pieces.

Here is the prompt:

"Turn this podcast transcript into 12 short social media posts. Each post should focus on one useful takeaway. Use plain English, a strong opening line, and keep each post under 80 words."

Then refine:

"Make 4 of them more story-driven."

"Make 4 of them more practical and direct."

"Turn 3 into carousel-style post outlines."

Now one long piece of content becomes multiple assets.

That is valuable because it saves time and increases the return on work the creator has already done

And beginner-friendly income often comes from exactly that:
not making something complicated,
but helping someone get more value out of what they already have.

Step-by-Step Action Plan

Now let's make this real.

Here is exactly what to do today.

Step 1: Choose one service to practice

Pick one:

- résumé summaries
- social media ideas
- product description rewrites
- transcript-to-post conversions

Do not choose four.
Choose one.

The fastest way to build confidence is through repetition on a single, clear task.

Step 2: Find one messy input

This could be:

- rough job notes
- a weak product listing

- a transcript from YouTube

- a local business page that clearly needs content ideas

- your own notes if nothing else is available

Messy input is good. That is what gives you something to improve.

Step 3: Run the four-step workflow

Use this sequence:

Give context

Explain the task, audience, goal, tone, and format.

Ask for options

Get 3–5 versions, not one.

Improve the result

Refine the best version for clarity, tone, and usefulness.

Human-check everything

Read it carefully, clean it up, and verify any factual claims.

Step 4: Save a before-and-after example

Create a simple document with:

- the original messy input

- the prompt you used

- the AI draft

- your final edited version

This matters because it gives you proof.

Not theoretical proof.

Actual proof that you can take something weak and make it stronger.

That is how belief starts becoming confidence.

Step 5: Build 3 reusable prompts

Create one prompt for drafting, one for improving, and one for simplifying.

Here is an example for product descriptions:

Draft prompt:

"Act as an Etsy copywriter. Write 3 product description options for this handmade item. Make them clear, warm, and customer-friendly."

Improve prompt:

"Improve this description so it sounds more natural and specific. Remove generic wording and make the product more appealing."

Simplify prompt:

"Rewrite this in plain English with shorter sentences and a more human tone."

These become your basic working tools.

Step 6: Practice on 3 examples

Do not wait for permission.

Do not wait for the perfect moment.

Practice on three different pieces of input.

You are not just learning AI here.

You are training your eye for what makes content clearer, stronger, and more useful.

Step 7: Turn it into a simple offer

Examples:

- "I will write 3 polished résumé summary options from your rough notes."
- "I will create 30 content ideas for your local business."
- "I will rewrite 10 Etsy product descriptions."
- "I will turn your transcript into 10 short social posts."

Keep the offer simple enough that someone understands it in seconds.

Step 8: Deliver with the same system every time

Do not reinvent your process every time.

Use the same reliable rhythm:

Draft. Edit. Verify.

That consistency is what makes beginner work feel more professional.

Common Mistakes to Avoid

1. Learning endlessly without practising

This feels safe, but it keeps you broke.

Watching more videos is not the same as building a usable skill.
You learn faster by doing one real transformation from messy to polished than by consuming three more hours of content.

2. Copying the first AI answer and calling it done

This is where bad reputations begin.

The first answer is usually raw.
Your job is to improve it.

3. Giving lazy instructions

Vague prompts lead to vague results.
The better your direction, the better your starting draft.

4. Delivering generic work

If the content could fit any business, any person, or any product, it is too broad.
Useful work sounds specific.

5. Trusting AI more than your own eyes

If something feels off, it probably is.
Read it carefully.
Check it.
Tighten it.

6. Offering too many things at once

Beginners often do this because they fear missing opportunities.
In reality, it makes them scattered.

One useful service is enough to start.

7. Forgetting what people are actually paying for

They are not paying for your prompt.

They are paying for the outcome:

less stress, better content, saved time, and a finished result.

Keep your focus there.

Quick Win Task

Here is what I want you to do today, not next week.

Pick one of these four:

Option 1: Take rough job notes and turn them into 3 résumé summary options.

Option 2: Create 20 social post ideas for a local business.

Option 3: Rewrite 3 weak product descriptions.

Option 4: Turn part of a transcript into 5 short posts.

Then follow this exact process:

Draft: Ask AI for a first version.

Edit: Ask for 3 versions or refinements.

Verify: Read the final version closely and improve it yourself.

When you are done, save:

- the original input
- the prompt
- the draft

- the final version

That simple exercise will teach you more than passive studying because it forces you to move from theory into results.

And that matters.

There is a big emotional difference between saying, "I'm trying to learn AI," and saying, "I took something messy and made it better."

The second one builds self-trust.

You do not need to become an AI expert to earn your first money with AI.

You need to become useful.

That is a smaller goal.
A more realistic goal.
And, for someone under pressure, a far more powerful goal.

Right now, there are people overwhelmed by rough notes, weak copy, empty content calendars, clunky descriptions, and long transcripts they do not know what to do with. They are not waiting for a genius. They are waiting for help.

That help can be simple.
And simple can still be valuable.

So stop telling yourself you need to know everything before you begin.

You do not.

You need one clear workflow.
One service you can practice.
One useful result you can point to.

That is how this starts.

Not with mastery.
With movement.

Not with complexity.
With usefulness.

Not with pretending to be advanced.
With learning just enough to solve a real problem for a real person.

That is how confidence grows.
That is how skill grows.
And very often, that is how the first money shows up, too.

You are closer than you think.

If you want, I can rewrite Chapter 6 next in the same stronger, more human style so the whole book stays consistent.

Chapter 6: Build a Simple Offer People Will Pay For

One of the biggest reasons people never make their first dollar online has nothing to do with talent.

It is not because they are too late.
It is not because they are too inexperienced.
It is not because they are bad with technology.

It is because they do not know what to offer.

So they stall.

They keep watching videos. Saving posts. Taking notes. Trying to "learn more" before they put themselves out there. On the surface, that looks productive. But underneath it, something else is usually happening:

They are scared to choose.

Because choosing means being visible.
Choosing means being judged.
Choosing means someone might ignore the offer—or worse, say no.

If that is where you are right now, let me say something that might take the pressure off:

Your first offer does not need to be brilliant.
It needs to be clear.

That is it.

You are not trying to impress the internet. You are trying to help one real person solve one annoying problem in a way that feels easy to buy.

That is how beginners start.
Not with a brand.
Not with a complicated funnel.
Not with some grand "AI agency."

They start with a simple offer a real human can understand in five seconds.

Because people do not buy effort.
They do not buy your stress.
They do not buy the fact that you spent three hours tweaking prompts.

They buy outcomes.

They buy relief.
They buy saved time.
They buy something that makes their life easier, faster, better, or less frustrating.

A small business owner does not want "AI-powered content assistance."
They want 15 social captions they can post this week.

A job seeker does not want "career optimisation support."

They want a résumé and cover letter that stop sounding weak and generic.

An online seller does not want "conversion-based e-commerce copy systems."

They want product descriptions done so they can finally list their items and move on.

That is the shift.

When you understand that, making your first offer becomes much less intimidating. You stop trying to sound impressive and start learning how to sound useful.

And useful gets paid.

Reality Check

Let's be honest about something.

Most first offers are bad.

Not because the person is stupid. Not because they have no potential. But beginners usually make their offer harder than it needs to be.

They either go too vague or too big.

Too vague sounds like this:

"I help businesses with AI."

"I offer AI consulting."

"I do digital growth solutions."

That may sound modern, but it does not sound buyable. It sounds blurry. Blurry offers do not make people reach for their wallets.

The other mistake is going too big:

"I can help with content, branding, lead generation, email marketing, automation, SEO, sales pages, social media, and strategy."

This sounds ambitious, but to a potential buyer, it often feels messy. It raises questions instead of answering them. It also creates a trap for you, because now you are promising a mountain of work before you have even built confidence.

Your first offer should not feel like hiring a department.
It should feel like buying one clear solution.

That matters even more when someone is careful with money.

And many of the people you will serve are careful with money.

They are small business owners doing ten jobs at once.
They are freelancers trying to stay visible online.
They are job seekers stressed about getting interviews.
They are creators sitting on content they never have time to repurpose.

These people are not usually asking, "Is this service sophisticated enough?"
They are asking:

What exactly am I getting?

Will this help me?

How fast can I get it?

Can I afford to try it?

Does this feel risky?

If your offer answers those questions quickly, you are already ahead of most beginners.

You do not need a perfect offer.

You need an understandable one.

Solution Breakdown

Why people buy outcomes, not effort

This is the foundation of everything.

People do not pay you because something took a long time.
They pay you because they want the result.

That sounds obvious, but many beginners still try to sell the wrong thing.

They talk about research.
They talk about the process.
They talk
They talk about how much care they put into the work.

None of that matters as much as they think it does.

Imagine a tired salon owner who has not posted on Instagram in two weeks. She is not thinking. *I really hope someone explains their creative workflow to me.* She is thinking, *Can somebody just give me posts I can use so this stops hanging over my head?*

Imagine a man applying for jobs late at night after work. He is not looking for "document enhancement." He is thinking, *I need my application to sound stronger because I cannot keep sending the same weak résumé everywhere.*

People buy the finished bridge, not the engineering notes.

That is why strong offers sound concrete.

Not:

"I provide AI-assisted content ideation."

But:

"I'll write 15 custom captions for your business."

Not:

"I help candidates position themselves better."

But:

"I'll rewrite your résumé and cover letter for one job target."

Not:

"I support e-commerce brands with copy."

But:

"I'll write 20 product descriptions for your online store."

Notice what changed. The second version is not fancier. It is simply clearer. You can picture it. You know what you are buying. That is what makes it stronger.

The anatomy of a beginner-friendly offer

A good first offer does six jobs at once. It tells the buyer:

Who it helps

What problem does it solve

What result does it deliver

How fast is it delivered

What it costs

Why does it feel safe to try

Let's walk through each one.

1. Who does it help

Your offer needs a face.

Not literally one person, but a clear type of person.

If you say your offer is for "everyone," it will feel like it is for no one.

Compare these:

"I help people with social media."
"I create ready-to-post captions for busy small business owners."

The second one lands harder because the right person sees themselves in it.

Other examples:

"I rewrite résumés and cover letters for job seekers applying to a specific role."
"I write product descriptions for online sellers who need listings

done fast."

"I turn podcasts and videos into social content for creators who do not have time to repurpose."

Specificity creates trust.

2. What problem does it solve?

Every good offer removes pain.

That pain does not have to be dramatic. It just has to be real.

Some examples:

"I never know what to post."
"My résumé sounds bland."
"I have products to upload, but writing the descriptions takes forever."
"I record good content, but I never turn it into more posts."
"I know I need a lead magnet, but I keep putting it off."

The more clearly you can name the frustration, the more your offer feels relevant.

People feel understood when you describe their problem in the words they would use themselves.

3. What result does it deliver?

This is where your offer becomes tangible.

A result is not "support."
A result is not "help."
A result is not "guidance."

A result is something they receive.

Examples:

15 custom social captions
A rewritten résumé and a tailored cover letter
20 product descriptions ready to upload
10 content pieces from one video or podcast
A one-page lead magnet or PDF guide

If the client cannot picture what they are getting, the offer is still too fuzzy.

4. How fast is it delivered?

Speed lowers resistance.

People feel more comfortable buying when they know the wait is not endless. A short turnaround also makes the service feel manageable.

Examples:

Delivered in 48 hours
Delivered in 3 days
First draft within 24 hours

You do not need to promise lightning speed if you cannot deliver it. In fact, do not. Broken promises are one of the fastest ways to lose confidence in yourself.

But a clear timeline helps people say yes.

5. What it costs

Your first offer should be easy to understand and easy to try.

Not dirt cheap.

Not randomly expensive.

Just fair.

You are not trying to squeeze every pound out of your first few clients. You are trying to get momentum, proof, and experience.

That means simple pricing works best.

One offer.

One price.

One defined result.

6. Why it feels low-risk

This part is easy to overlook, but it matters.

People buy faster when the offer feels safe.

A safe offer is:

Small enough to understand

Specific enough to trust

Limited enough to feel manageable

Clear enough to compare against the price

Supported by a sample

That last one can change everything.

If you do not have testimonials yet, you can still build trust with examples.

Why your first offer should be simple, not impressive

There is a trap many smart beginners fall into.

They think simple looks amateur.

So they try to sound bigger than they are.

They use formal language. Complicated service names. Long packages. Fancy descriptions that make the work sound more advanced.

But buyers do not reward complexity.
They reward clarity.

A simple offer is easier to buy because it's easier to understand.

Think about the difference between these two:

"I provide AI-driven Omni-channel messaging systems for emerging brands."

"I'll turn one of your videos into 10 social posts you can publish this week."

The second one wins.

Not because it sounds more intelligent.
Because it sounds more real.

People trust what they can picture.

Your first offer should not make someone say, "That sounds impressive."
It should make them say, "Oh, I need that."

How to make an offer small, clear, and low-risk

The easiest way to improve your first offer is to shrink it.

Beginners often assume they need to offer more to justify charging. Usually, the opposite is true. When you narrow the offer, it becomes more believable and easier to deliver.

Instead of:

"I'll manage your content."

Try:

"I'll create 15 custom captions for your small business."

Instead of:

"I help people improve their job applications."

Try:

"I'll rewrite your résumé and cover letter for one job target."

Instead of:

"I do e-commerce copy."

Try:

"I'll write 20 product descriptions for your online store."

Instead of:

"I help creators grow online."

Try:

"I'll turn your podcast episode into 10 ready-to-post content pieces."

A smaller offer does three useful things:

It makes the buying decision easier.

It helps you deliver without chaos.

It reduces the chance of disappointing someone.

That is exactly what you want when you are starting.

Packaging AI-assisted work in a way that feels valuable

Here is a mistake to avoid:

Do not make the service about the AI.

The client is not paying for access to ChatGPT. They can open a tool themselves. What they are paying for is the result you create with it.

That includes:

Knowing what to ask

Giving the right context

Sorting through weak output

Editing until it sounds natural

Matching the tone to the client

Removing fluff

Checking for errors

Turning a rough draft into something useful

That is the value.

AI is part of the engine. It is not the product.

So instead of saying, "I use AI to create content," frame it like this:

"I create ready-to-use content tailored to your business, voice, and goals."

That sounds more valuable because it focuses on what the buyer receives.

And it is honest.

Because raw AI output is rarely worth paying for.
Thoughtful, shaped, human-checked output is.

Using samples instead of credentials

This matters a lot if you are nervous because you have no experience.

You do not need to wait until someone "gives you a chance."
You can create proof before your first client ever appears.

That proof is called a sample.

A sample is a small example of the exact result you are offering.

If you want to sell captions, write a few sample captions.
If you want to sell résumé rewrites, create a before-and-after example.
If you want to sell product descriptions, write three of them.
If you want to sell content repurposing, take one transcript and turn it into several posts.
If you want to sell lead magnets, build a one-page PDF for a sample business.

Think about how much more confident you would feel messaging someone if you could say, "I put together a sample so you can see the style."

Now think about the buyer.

They may not know you.

They may not care about your background.

They may not have time to read a long explanation.

But they can look at a sample in thirty seconds and decide whether the work feels promising.

That is powerful.

In the beginning, samples are often more useful than credentials because they answer the only question that really matters:

Can you actually do this?

Pricing without panic

Pricing can make otherwise capable people fall apart.

Not because pricing is complicated, but because it feels emotional.

The moment you name a price, it can feel like you are putting a number on your value as a person. So you hesitate. You apologize. You undercharge. You say, "I don't know, whatever you think is fair."

Do not do that.

You are not pricing your worth.
You are pricing a defined result.

That distinction will help you more than you realise.

For a first offer, fixed pricing is usually easier than hourly pricing. It keeps the conversation cleaner and removes uncertainty.

Here are realistic beginner ranges for small, defined offers:

15 custom captions: £25 to £60

Résumé and cover letter for one job target: £35 to £80

20 product descriptions: £30 to £75

10 repurposed content pieces from one video or podcast: £40 to £90

One-page lead magnet or PDF guide: £40 to £100

These are starting points, not laws. Your skill, speed, and niche will influence where you land. But the bigger lesson is this:

Do not try to invent a price out of panic.

Match the price to the outcome and the scope.

A useful line you can borrow is:

"My starter rate for this is £X. That includes [deliverable] delivered in [time frame]."

No apology.

No rambling.

No defensive explanation.

Clear prices build trust.

Step-by-Step Action Plan

Now let's build your first offer in a practical way.

Do not treat this like a theory. Do it as you read.

By the end of this section, you should have something you could actually show another person.

Step 1: Choose one problem you can solve right now

Not the most impressive one.

Not the one you might be good at six months from now.

Choose one problem you can help solve this week.

Good beginner examples:

Social captions for small businesses

Résumé and cover letter rewriting

Product descriptions for online sellers

Content repurposing from video or podcast episodes

A simple one-page PDF guide or lead magnet

Pick the one that feels most doable with the tools and skills you already have.

Ask yourself:

Can I create a useful result with AI help?

Can I finish the work in a reasonable amount of time?

Can I explain the offer in one sentence?

If the answer is yes, keep going.

Step 2: Decide exactly who the offer is for

Use this sentence:

"I help [specific person] who needs [specific result]."

Examples:

I help small business owners who need ready-to-post social content.

I help job seekers who want stronger applications for one role.

I help online sellers who need product descriptions written faster.

I help creators turn long content into short posts they can actually use.

This step matters because the clearer the person, the stronger the message.

Step 3: Write down the pain in everyday language

Use this sentence:

"They are struggling because…"

Finish it honestly.

Examples:

They are struggling because writing captions keeps falling to the bottom of the to-do list.
They are struggling because their résumé sounds generic and forgettable.
They are struggling because listing products takes too much time.
They are struggling because they create long-form content once and never reuse it.

This gives your offer emotional weight. It stops you from sounding generic.

Step 4: Turn it into one clean offer sentence

Use this format:

"I'll help [who] by delivering [specific result] in [time frame] for [price]."

Examples:

I'll create 15 custom social captions for your small business in 48 hours for £35.

I'll rewrite your résumé and cover letter for one job target in 3 days for £50.

I'll write 20 product descriptions for your online store in 48 hours for £45.

I'll turn your podcast or video into 10 ready-to-post content pieces in 3 days for £60.

I'll create a one-page lead magnet or PDF guide for your business in 3 days for £75.

That sentence alone can become a post, a DM, a gig title, or the basis of your profile.

Step 5: Make one to three samples

Do not wait for a client before proving you can do the work.

Create proof first.

Here is what that can look like.

If your offer is social captions

Pick a local business, a friend's business, or a made-up example.

Write:

3 to 5 sample captions

a mix of styles, such as promotional, helpful, or community-focused

a short note showing how you matched the tone

If your offer is résumé rewriting

Create:

One weak "before" section

One stronger "after" section

A sample opening paragraph for a tailored cover letter

If your offer is product descriptions

Choose three sample products and write:

A product title

A benefit-led description

A few bullets if relevant

If your offer is content repurposing

Take a video transcript, podcast excerpt, or article and turn it into:

3 short social posts

2 hooks

1 quote

1 email idea

If your offer is a lead magnet or PDF guide

Create a one-page guide on a simple topic, such as:

5 Ways a Local Café Can Get More Repeat Customers

3 Resume Mistakes That Quietly Cost You Interviews

4 Easy Instagram Post Ideas for Busy Service Businesses

Keep it clean. Useful. Easy to skim.

The point is not perfection.

The point is evidence.

Step 6: Set a starter price

Choose a price that feels fair, slightly uncomfortable, and believable.

That balance matters.

If it is too low, you may attract people who do not respect the work.
If it is too high, you may avoid promoting it because you do not believe it yourself.

For most people, the right starting price is the one they can say out loud without shrinking.

Pick it.

Write it down.

Stop renegotiating with yourself every ten minutes.

Step 7: Write a simple message you can actually send

You do not need a website.

You do not need branding.

You need words you can use.

Here is a simple template:

"Hi, I'm offering a done-for-you service for [type of person]. I help with [problem]. My starter offer is [deliverable], delivered in [time frame], for [price]. I've put together a sample as well, happy to send it over."

That works because it is short, clear, and low-pressure.

Step 8: Make the next step obvious

Do not end your offer with confusion.

Tell people exactly what to do next.

Examples:

"Send me your business type and brand tone."
"Send me the job link you are applying to."
"Send me your product list or store link."
"Send me the video, podcast link, or transcript."

The easier the next step feels, the easier it is for someone to say yes.

Sample Offers

These are strong starting points because they are easy to understand, easy to deliver, and tied to visible outcomes.

"I'll create 15 custom social captions for your small business"

This is ideal for small business owners who know they should post but keep putting it off. You are solving the problem of inconsistency and time pressure. They receive 15 captions they can actually use, and the offer is simple enough to explain in one line.

"I'll rewrite your résumé and cover letter for one job target"

This works because it connects to a real emotional need. Job seekers are often stressed, discouraged, and tired of sending weak applications. A tailored résumé and cover letter feel valuable because they speak directly to a goal the buyer already cares deeply about.

"I'll write 20 product descriptions for your online store"

This is a practical offer for sellers who have products ready but cannot stand writing the copy. It removes repetitive work, saves time, and creates an obvious finished result.

"I'll turn your video or podcast into 10 ready-to-post content pieces"

This is a strong offer for creators, coaches, and small business owners who already have useful content but are not getting enough mileage out of it. You help them stretch one asset further without more recording.

"I'll create a one-page lead magnet or PDF guide for your business"

This works well for service businesses that need something useful to offer potential clients or email subscribers. The result feels tangible.

They are not buying "marketing help." They are buying a finished asset.

Common Mistakes to Avoid

Offering too much too early

This is one of the easiest ways to make your first offer harder to sell and harder to deliver.

When you are nervous, it feels tempting to add more. More pages. More edits. More strategy. More extras. But overloaded offers often create confusion, not value.

Keep your first offer narrow.
Let it work before you expand it.

Using vague language like "AI consulting"

Most people do not wake up wanting "AI consulting."

They want a task done.
They want a result.
They want something off their plate.

If your offer sounds abstract, modern, and hard to picture, simplify it until a tired stranger could understand it instantly.

Competing on the lowest possible price

Being cheap is not the same as being attractive.

Rock-bottom pricing can make people question the quality. It can also pull in difficult buyers who want too much and value too little.

You do not need to be the cheapest.

You need to be the clearest, most useful option.

Creating an offer nobody understands in five seconds

This is the test.

Could someone read your offer once and know what you do?

If not, keep rewriting.

Clarity is not a cosmetic improvement.
It is the sales mechanism.

Quick Win Task

Do this today before you move on.

Not tomorrow. Not when you feel more ready.

Today.

Write your first offer using this format:

I help [who] by delivering [result] in [time frame] for [price].

Then create one sample to support it.

After that, write one short message you could send to a potential buyer.

Use this:

"Hi, I'm offering a simple done-for-you service for [type of person]. I help with [problem]. My starter offer is [deliverable], delivered in [time frame], for [price]. I've also made a sample and can send it over if useful."

That is enough to get moving.

You do not need a full business setup to start acting like someone who has something worth selling.

You need one clear offer and one example.

That is a real beginning.

A lot of people stay stuck because they think the breakthrough will come from finding the perfect idea.

Usually, it does not.

Usually, it comes from making a simple decision and putting something clear in front of another human being.

That is what this chapter is really about.

Not just offers.
Momentum.

Because once you build a clear offer, something shifts.

You stop feeling like someone "trying to figure it out."
You start becoming someone with a service.

That matters more than it sounds.

The first time you can say, clearly, "This is what I do, this is who it helps, and this is what it costs," your confidence changes. The work becomes real. The possibility becomes real.

And no, your first offer will not be perfect.

It may be too cheap.
It may need tightening.
It may attract the wrong person once or twice.
You may rewrite it ten times before it clicks.

That is normal.

What matters is that you stop hiding behind preparation and start building something people can actually buy.

Remember this:

Simple sells.
Clear wins.
Small offers create momentum.

You do not need to look impressive.
You need to be useful.

That is how the first income starts.

Quietly. Practically. One solved problem at a time.

Chapter 7: Get Your First Buyer Without an Audience, Website, or Following

Most beginners think their first buyer will come after they look more "legit."

After the website is finished.

After the Instagram page looks polished.

After they post for a few months.

After they feel more confident.

After they know exactly what to say.

So they wait.

And while they wait, nothing happens.

No buyers.

No proof.

No momentum.

No money.

Here is the truth: most people do not realise until much later that their first buyer usually does not come from content. It comes from contact.

It comes from a message.

A conversation.

A simple offer made to the right person at the right time.

That is good news, especially if money feels tight and you do not have months to "build a brand" before earning anything.

You do not need an audience to get paid.

You do not need a website to get paid.

You do not need followers to get paid.

You need to find someone with a problem you can help solve and make it easy for them to say yes.

That is what this chapter is about.

Not how to look impressive.

How to get useful enough, brave enough, and clear enough to win your first buyer.

Reality Check

Let's be honest. Reaching out to people can feel uncomfortable.

You may worry about sounding awkward.

You may worry about being ignored.

You may worry that people will think, "Who is this person, and why are they messaging me?"

Under all of that is usually one deeper fear: rejection.

Not just "What if they say no?"
But "What if they say no because I'm not good enough?"

That fear keeps a lot of smart people stuck.

They tell themselves they are "preparing."
But often, they are hiding.

They are tweaking logos, watching more videos, rewriting their offer again, and waiting to feel ready.

Ready is overrated.

Most first clients are not won by people who feel fully confident. They are won by people who are willing to act while still feeling nervous.

And here is the other truth: outreach is only painful when you think of it as asking strangers for a favour.

That is not what you are doing.

You are not begging.
You are not bothering people.
You are not tricking anyone.

You are noticing a problem and offering help.

That is a completely different energy.

The people who get clients fastest are not always the most experienced. They are usually the ones who stop making this bigger than it is.

They keep it simple.

"I noticed something you could improve."

"I had an idea that might help."

"I can show you an example if you want."

That is not pushy. That is useful.

Your first buyer is rarely looking for the most polished person on the internet. They are usually looking for someone who understands their problem and can help them fix it without wasting their time.

Solution Breakdown

Why your first buyer usually comes from direct outreach, not content

Content can help later. It can build trust. It can show your style. It can bring people to you over time.

But "over time" is the key phrase.

When you are trying to make your first money, content can move too slowly. You can post for weeks and hear almost nothing. Not because you are bad, but because attention takes time to build.

Outreach is faster because it puts you in front of real people now.

Instead of hoping the right person finds your post, you find the right person and start the conversation yourself.

That matters when your goal is not to become an influencer. Your goal is to get one buyer.

Think about the difference.

Content says, "I'm here if you happen to see me."

Outreach says, "I saw your situation, and I think I can help."

One is passive. One is active.

When you are starting from zero, activity usually wins.

The fastest places to find beginner-friendly buyers

You do not need to search the whole internet. You just need a few places where problems are easy to spot, and buyers are easy to reach.

Friends and extended network

This is the easiest place to start, even though many people resist it.

Why? Because it feels personal. It can feel embarrassing to tell people you are offering a service.

But your first buyer does not have to be a stranger.

It might be:

- a friend who is job hunting
- a cousin who runs a small business
- someone from a previous job
- a parent from your child's school
- a friend of a friend who posts online for their business
- someone you already know who needs help but has never had the time to fix the problem

This is often the fastest route because trust already exists.

You do not need to give a polished pitch. You just need to explain what you help with in plain English.

Local businesses

Local businesses are one of the best opportunities for beginners because the problems are usually obvious.

They are busy.
They wear too many hats.
They know they should market better, but it stays at the bottom of the list.

Look at:

- cafes
- salons
- barbers
- gyms
- cleaners
- estate agents
- dog groomers
- dentists
- tradespeople
- restaurants
- coaches
- photographers
- accountants

Many of them have one or more of these issues:

- weak social media captions
- inconsistent posting
- outdated profile descriptions
- unclear offers
- no obvious call to action
- poor website wording
- no follow-up emails
- wasted content that could be reused better

That is an opportunity.

Job seekers

Job seekers are often willing to pay for help because the pain is immediate. They are trying to get interviews, and they know weak applications cost them chances.

They may need:

- a stronger resume
- a better LinkedIn profile
- tailored cover letters
- clearer achievement-based bullet points
- interview preparation materials

This market works well because the result is easy to understand: present me better so I can get more responses.

Creators and freelancers

Small creators and solo business owners often have plenty of ideas and not enough time.

They may need:

- captions
- content repurposing
- hooks
- post ideas
- email drafts
- lead magnets
- simple sales copy
- client onboarding documents

A creator may post one good video and then move on, even though that one video could become five more pieces of content. A freelancer may be great at their craft but terrible at explaining their offer online.

You do not need to invent a need. The need is already there.

Online communities

Facebook groups, niche forums, Slack communities, Discord servers, and sub-reddits can show you what people are struggling with in real time.

The mistake is jumping in and pitching too soon.

Instead, watch what people complain about. Watch the questions that keep coming up. Pay attention to repeated frustrations.

When the same pain keeps appearing, that is where an offer can live.

For example:

- small business owners saying they never know what to post
- job seekers asking if their resume is good enough
- creators saying they cannot keep up with content
- freelancers struggling to explain their services clearly

Problems tell you where money is.

Freelance marketplaces are used strategically.

Freelance marketplaces are not always the best place to build a long-term business, but they can help you get your first win if you use them well.

The mistake beginners make is applying it to everything.

A better approach:

- look for small jobs
- apply to recent posts
- target simple deliverables
- personalise each proposal
- focus on jobs where the outcome is clear

For example, "Rewrite my LinkedIn summary" is better than "Help me with my whole brand strategy."

Clarity makes it easier to win.

How to find people with obvious problems you can solve

Your life gets much easier when you stop trying to sell to everyone and start looking for people whose problems are already visible.

Visible problems are gold.

You go on a local business Instagram page and see great photos with flat, forgettable captions.
You look at a job seeker's LinkedIn, and the headline says almost nothing meaningful.
You find a creator posting solid videos but leaving every caption empty or weak.
You visit a service business website and still have no idea what they actually offer or why someone should choose them.

Now your message does not feel random. It feels relevant.

This is why "I noticed…" works so well.

"I'm offering…" starts with your service.
"I noticed…" starts with their reality.

That difference matters.

Compare these two openings.

"Hi, I offer AI content services for businesses."

Versus:

"Hi, I noticed your page looks professional, but the captions are not really giving people a reason to book or message."

The first sounds like a pitch.
The second sounds like a person paying attention.

That is what you want.

Warm outreach vs cold outreach for beginners

Warm outreach is reaching out to people who already know you, know of you, or have some connection to you.

Cold outreach is contacting people who have no connection to you at all.

If you are a beginner, warm outreach is usually the easier place to begin.

Why?
Because people are more likely to respond.
Because the conversation feels more natural.
Because you do not need to "prove yourself" as hard.
Because it helps you build confidence before moving into colder leads.

Warm outreach can include:

- friends
- old co-workers
- family contacts
- mutuals
- people in your local area
- people you have already interacted with online

Cold outreach can still work very well. But if you are nervous, do not make it harder than it needs to be. Start where the trust gap is smaller.

How to write a message that does not feel pushy or awkward

A good outreach message is not clever. It is clear.

Most strong messages include five simple parts:

1. A short greeting
2. One thing you noticed
3. A useful thought or suggestion
4. A small offer or example
5. A low-pressure close

That is enough.

You do not need to explain your whole background.
You do not need to write three paragraphs.
You do not need to mention every service you could possibly offer.

The more nervous people feel, the more they tend to over-explain.

But buyers do not need your life story. They need to quickly understand one thing: can this person help me with a problem I care about?

Also, do not make AI the star of the message.

People are not buying "AI." They are buying a better result.

They want:

- more inquiries
- stronger applications
- cleaner messaging

- more content from the same effort
- less wasted time
- better positioning

Focus on that.

Why "I noticed…" is more powerful than "I'm offering…"

This shift is small, but it changes the entire tone of your outreach.

"I'm offering…" is centred on you.

"I noticed…" is centred on them.

That means the message feels less like a sales pitch and more like a real observation.

It also proves you did not blast the same message to fifty people.

People respond better when they feel seen.

You are not saying, "Please buy my service."
You are saying, "I saw something specific, and I think there may be a simple way to improve it."

That feels more thoughtful. More human. More trustworthy.

Using a free sample or mini audit to open conversations

One of the easiest ways to make someone feel safe saying yes is to remove some of the risk.

A free sample or mini audit can do that.

Examples:

- rewrite one social caption
- improve one resume bullet point
- suggest three stronger content hooks
- rewrite a weak headline on a homepage
- point out three missed opportunities on a business profile
- turn one video into three repurposed post ideas

This works because it gives the other person a glimpse of what working with you would feel like.

It says, "You do not have to guess whether I can help. Here is a small example."

That said, there is a line.

A sample should build trust, not drain your time.

Do not rewrite the whole website for free.
Do not rebuild the entire resume for free.
Do not create two weeks of free content hoping they will later pay.

Give enough to spark interest. Not enough to replace the paid work.

Following up without sounding desperate

Most beginners give up too early.

They send a few messages, hear nothing back, and immediately assume the market is not interested.

Usually, that is not true.

People are busy. Messages get buried. Someone sees your note while standing in line, means to reply later, and forgets.

A follow-up is not desperate if it is calm and useful.

Good follow-up:

"Hi, just circling back in case this got buried. Happy to send over a quick example if that helps."

That is easy to read and easy to answer.

Bad follow-up:

"Just checking again, I'd really love to work with you and can start today and also lower my rate…"

That feels anxious, and anxiety is not persuasive.

Follow up once or twice. Keep it short. Keep it light. Then move on.

Step-by-Step Action Plan

Here is how to put this into practice without getting overwhelmed.

Step 1: Pick one small offer

Do not try to sell five services at once. Choose one thing that is easy to explain and easy to deliver.

Examples:

- 15 custom captions for local businesses
- resume and LinkedIn rewrite for job seekers
- content repurposing for creators
- welcome email sequence for freelancers
- Google Business profile rewrite for local service businesses

A simple offer beats a broad one.

You want someone to understand it in seconds.

For example:

"I help local businesses improve their social media captions so more people message or book."

Or:

"I help job seekers rewrite their resumes and LinkedIn so they sound stronger and get more interviews."

Simple is stronger than impressive.

Step 2: Choose one type of buyer

Do not jump between local businesses, coaches, creators, and job seekers all at once.

Pick one group first.

This makes your outreach sharper and your learning faster.

Ask yourself:

- Who can I help most easily?
- Whose problem do I understand?
- Who feels least intimidating to message?

That is your starting point.

Step 3: Find 20 people with obvious problems

Your job is not to find perfect leads. Your job is to find people with visible room for improvement.

Create a list of 20 names.

For each person, write down:

- name
- business or role
- where you found them
- the problem you noticed
- whether you messaged them
- whether they replied

Examples of visible problems:

- a salon posting lovely photos with weak captions
- a freelancer's website with confusing wording
- a job seeker with bland resume bullet points
- a creator posting useful videos but not reusing them anywhere else

This step matters because good outreach starts with good targeting.

Step 4: Write one short message using the "I noticed…" approach

Your message should sound like a human being, not a template machine.

A simple structure:

"Hi [Name], I came across your [page/profile/site] and noticed [specific problem]. I think [small improvement] could help with [result]. If useful, I'd be happy to send over [tiny sample/example]. No pressure."

That is enough.

Step 5: Personalise each message

Even one sentence of personalisation can change the entire feel.

Mention:

- a recent post
- a specific page
- a detail about their content
- the exact problem you noticed

This is what separates thoughtful outreach from spam.

Step 6: Offer a small sample

Make it easy for them to say yes without committing money immediately.

For example:

- "I can send you one example caption."
- "I can rewrite one bullet point so you can compare."
- "I can show you how I'd turn one video into three posts."
- "I can send a better headline idea for your homepage."

The smaller the next step, the easier the reply.

Step 7: Send your first 10 messages

This is where most people stall. They think about outreach more than they do it.

Do not aim for perfection. Aim for sent.

Send 10 good messages. Not one. Not three. Ten.

A single ignored message means nothing. A small batch gives you real feedback.

Step 8: Follow up after two days

If someone has not replied, send a gentle follow-up.

Keep it short:
"Hi [Name], just wanted to follow up in case this got buried. Happy to send a quick example if helpful."

That is enough.

Step 9: Pay attention to what gets responses

After 10 to 20 messages, patterns usually appear.

You may notice:

- local businesses respond more than creators
- "I noticed…" performs better than "I help…"
- people react better to samples than general offers
- shorter messages get more replies

Do not guess. Learn from the market.

Step 10: Improve and repeat

Your first round is not about perfection. It is about information.

After every batch, ask:

- Which messages got replies?
- Which offers felt easiest to explain?
- Which buyer type seemed most interested?
- Was my message too long?
- Was my offer too vague?

Then adjust and send the next batch.

This is how first buyers happen. Not from magic. From repetition, clarity, and small improvements.

Scripts and Examples

Use these as a starting point, then make them sound like you.

Simple DM template for local businesses

Hi [Name], I came across your page and noticed your photos look great, but the captions are very brief and do not really guide people toward booking or messaging.

A few stronger captions with clearer calls to action could probably help turn more profile visits into real inquiries.

If helpful, I can send over one example caption so you can see what I mean. No pressure.

Offer message for job seekers.

Hi [Name], I saw that you're applying for jobs at the moment. I had a quick look at your profile/resume style, and I think your experience may be underselling you.

A clearer, more achievement-focused version could help you come across much stronger.

If you want, I can rewrite one bullet point or part of your summary as a sample so you can compare it.

Reaching out to small creators who need content repurposing

Hi [Name], I checked out your content and noticed you're sharing genuinely useful ideas, but each piece seems to be doing only one job.

A lot of your posts could probably be turned into multiple short captions, hooks, or follow-up pieces, so you get more reach from the same work.

If useful, I can mock up three repurposed ideas from one of your recent posts.

Referral message to personal contacts

Hey [Name], quick one. I've started helping [type of person] with [specific result], like [simple example].

If you know anyone who might need help with that, I'd really appreciate an introduction. I'm keeping it simple and affordable while I build up case studies.

No pressure at all. Just wanted to mention it.

Common Mistakes to Avoid

1. Sending copy-paste spam

People know when they are one of fifty.

You do not need to write a custom essay for every person, but you do need to show that you actually looked at their situation.

One real observation goes further than a polished generic pitch.

2. Talking about AI instead of the outcome

This is one of the fastest ways to lose people.

Most buyers do not care what tool you use. They care what gets better.

Do not say:

"I use AI to streamline content creation."

Say:

"I can turn one video into five short posts you can use this week."

That feels concrete. That feels useful.

3. Giving away too much free work

A free sample should build trust, not become unpaid labour.

One caption is fine.
One bullet point is fine.
One quick audit is fine.

A full website rewrite for free is not fine.

Protect your energy. Your generosity should help you open doors, not exhaust you.

4. Quitting too early

Five messages is not outreach. It is barely a start.

A lot of beginners stop before the process has had any real chance to work. They interpret a few ignored messages as proof they failed.

It is not proof. It is part of the process.

Sometimes your first buyer comes from message twelve. Sometimes from message twenty-three. Sometimes from a follow-up, not the original message.

Keep going.

5. Making the message too long

Long messages usually come from nerves.

You are trying to sound credible, so you explain everything.

But long messages feel heavy. People skim them. Then ignore them.

Short, clear, relevant messages get more replies.

6. Trying to sound overly professional

You do not need stiff business language.

You need to sound clear, calm, and real.

A natural message beats a corporate-sounding one almost every time, especially with small businesses and individuals.

7. Targeting people with no visible need

Do not waste time pitching people who already look highly polished or clearly do not need what you offer.

Find the people where the gap is obvious.

That is where your chance is highest.

Quick Win Task

Do this today before you overthink it.

Choose one offer.
Choose one buyer type.
Then complete these five steps:

1. Write your offer in one sentence.
Example: "I help local businesses improve their social captions so more people inquire or book."

2. Find 10 people with an obvious problem.
Not random people. People you can genuinely help.

3. Write one simple message using the "I noticed…" format.

4. Personalise it and send it to all 10.

5. Offer a tiny sample to anyone who responds.

That is your job today.

Not buying a domain.
Not making a logo.

Not watching more videos.

Not trying to look important online.

Just this.

If you do this properly, you will already be ahead of most beginners, because most beginners never actually ask for the work.

They stay in preparation mode.

You are trying to enter earning mode.

Your first buyer is probably not waiting for you to become more polished.

They are waiting for you to become more direct.

They are already out there.
A local business owner who knows their marketing is weak.
A job seeker is tired of sending applications into silence.
A creator who is stretched thin and wasting good content.
A freelancer whose online presence is costing them work.

These people do not need you to be famous.
They do not need you to have ten thousand followers.
They do not need a perfect website.

They need help.

And that is what should give you confidence.

Not your logo.
Not your bio.
Not how "professional" you look.

Your confidence should come from usefulness.

If you can solve a real problem, even in a small way, you have something valuable.

Will some people ignore you? Yes.
Will some people say no? Of course.
Will some messages feel awkward at first? Absolutely.

But none of that means you are doing it wrong.

It means you are in the game.

And that is where momentum begins.

One message turns into one reply.
One reply turns into one conversation.
One conversation turns into one paid job.
One paid job turns into proof.
And proof changes how you see yourself.

You stop being someone who hopes this might work.

You become someone who knows it can.

So send the messages.

Not when you feel fearless.
Not when your brand is finished.
Not when everything looks perfect.

Send them while it still feels uncomfortable.

Because that discomfort is often the doorway to your first real result.

Chapter 8: Deliver Results Fast: How to Do the Work Even as a Beginner

Getting a client feels exciting for about five minutes.

Then the panic kicks in.

Now it is real. Someone said yes. Someone is trusting you. Someone expects you to deliver something useful, and suddenly, every doubt you have been carrying gets louder.

What if I mess this up?
What if they can tell I'm new?
What if the work isn't good enough?

If you are in that headspace, you are not weak. You are normal.

Most beginners do not struggle because they are lazy or incapable. They struggle because the moment money gets involved, the work starts to feel heavier. The pressure rises. They overthink small decisions. They keep tweaking things that are already fine. They chase perfection because they are scared that "good enough" will expose them.

But here is what matters:

Your first clients are not looking for perfection. They are looking for help.

They want the résumé fixed.

They want the captions written.

They want the product descriptions cleaned up.

They want the video turned into content.

They want one less thing sitting unfinished on their plate.

That is where your opportunity is.

You do not need to be brilliant. You do not need to be the best person in your niche. You do not need ten years of experience.

You need to be useful.

You need to take a problem that feels messy to them and turn it into something clear, finished, and usable.

That is what gets you paid.

That is what gets you remembered.

That is what turns a first job into a second one.

This chapter is about how to do exactly that, even if you still feel like a beginner.

Reality Check

A lot of people imagine paid work as some high-level, polished performance.

It usually is not.

Especially at the beginning.

Your early clients often don't hire you because they believe you are the greatest talent they have ever seen. They are hiring you because they have a task they do not want to do themselves. They want it off their plate, handled, and they want progress.

That is why beginner clients do not need perfection. They need useful results.

A local business owner who needs captions is not asking for a Pulitzer Prize. They need words they can post this week.

A job seeker who hires you to improve a résumé does not need genius-level copywriting. They need a stronger document that gives them a better shot.

A creator who wants a YouTube video turned into written content is not asking you to reinvent their brand. They want help turning one piece of content into several.

This matters because perfectionism is one of the fastest ways to lose money as a beginner.

You spend three hours trying to improve something that was already strong enough in ninety minutes. You miss deadlines because you keep editing. You create stress for yourself over tiny details that the client may never even notice.

Meanwhile, the client usually cares most about three things:

Did you understand what I needed?
Did you make my life easier?
Did you deliver on time?

That is the real game.

Not looking impressive.
Not sounding advanced.
Not pretending you have everything figured out.

Just solving the problem in front of you, cleanly and calmly.

And here is the part most beginners miss: when you do that well, clients often assume you are more experienced than you are.

Not because you used complicated language.
Because you were easy to work with.

Solution Breakdown

When you are new, the best thing you can do is stop reinventing your process every time. You need a simple framework you can use for almost any client job.

Here it is:

1. Clarify the task

Do not start by opening AI.
Do not start by "seeing what happens."
Do not start by guessing.

Start by getting clear.

What exactly does the client want?
What is the final deliverable?
What should it help them achieve?

What tone, style, or format do they want?

When do they need it?

A vague project can become stressful very quickly. Most beginner mistakes happen here. People accept unclear instructions because they fear sounding inexperienced. Then they build the wrong thing and spend their energy later fixing avoidable problems.

Asking clear questions does not make you sound new. It makes you sound responsible.

2. Gather the raw material

AI works best when you feed it something real.

That means your job is not to hope the tool magically knows what the client means. Your job is to gather the ingredients.

If it is a résumé, you need past roles, achievements, and target jobs.
If it is captions, you need the offer, the audience, the tone, and examples.
If it is product descriptions, you need features, benefits, customer type, and brand style.
If it is content repurposing, you need the video, transcript, audience, and platform.

Weak input creates weak output. Every time.

3. Use AI to create a draft

Now AI becomes useful.

Not as a substitute for you. As a speed tool.

Use it to generate a first version quickly. Use it to organise messy ideas. Use it to rewrite, simplify, expand, shorten, and give you options.

But remember this: the first draft is not the finished product. It is the beginning.

A lot of people make the mistake of treating AI output like a completed job. That is usually where mediocre work comes from.

4. Edit for accuracy and tone

This is where your value becomes obvious.

You review the work and ask:

Is this actually correct?
Does this sound natural?
Is it too generic?
Does it fit the client's voice, brand, or goal?
Did anything weird slip in?

The difference between average work and solid work is often one careful human review.

5. Deliver cleanly and on time

A good result can still feel disappointing if the delivery is sloppy.

If the file names are messy, the formatting is ugly, and the handoff message is unclear, the work feels less valuable even if the content is decent.

Clients notice the whole experience.

A clean delivery tells them, "You made the right choice."

That matters more than most beginners realise.

Step-by-Step Action Plan

Let's make this practical.

Here is how to complete a paid job without spiralling, stalling, or sending something half-baked.

Step 1: Define what "done well" actually means

Before you do anything, write one sentence:

This project is successful if…

That sentence forces you to focus on the result instead of getting lost in unnecessary polishing.

Examples:

This project is successful if the client gets a résumé that sounds stronger, cleaner, and more targeted to the jobs they want.

This project is successful if the client receives 15 social captions they can post with little to no editing.

This project is successful if the product descriptions clearly explain the product and make it more appealing to a buyer.

This project is successful if the video is turned into useful written content that the client can publish across platforms.

You would be surprised how much stress disappears when you define success clearly.

A lot of overthinking comes from not knowing what you are aiming at.

Step 2: Ask smart questions early

This is one of the easiest ways to look professional fast.

You do not need a giant questionnaire. You just need a few questions that remove confusion.

A simple message like this works well:

"Thanks again. Before I start, I want to make sure I shape this in the most useful way for you. Could you send me:

- the current version or raw material
- who this is for
- the tone or style you want
- any examples you like
- your preferred deadline or delivery time"

That sounds calm, clear, and competent.

You are not apologising for being new. You are making sure the work is right.

Here are a few strong questions you can use in almost any project:

"What would make this feel like a win for you?"

"Who is the audience for this?"

"Do you want this to sound more professional, more conversational, or more persuasive?"

"Do you have an example of something similar that you like?"

"What format would be easiest for you to receive?"

Those questions save time because they get to the real goal.

And that matters, because many clients do not communicate clearly the first time. They know they want something better. They do not always know how to describe it. Part of your job is helping them get specific.

Step 3: Organise the information before you use AI

Do not throw a pile of messy notes into AI and hope it turns into something strong.

Take a few minutes to sort the raw material first.

If you are rewriting a résumé, separate it into:

- contact info
- target role
- work history
- achievements
- skills
- education

If you are writing captions, sort them into:

- product or service
- audience pain points
- key benefits

- tone of voice
- call to action

If you are doing product descriptions, gather:

- product name
- features
- benefits
- materials or specs
- ideal buyer
- brand tone

This step feels small, but it changes everything. Better structure gives you better prompts. Better prompts give you better drafts. Better drafts mean less editing later.

That is how you get faster without getting sloppy.

Step 4: Use AI like a collaborator, not a crutch

A bad prompt produces bad work. A vague prompt produces generic work.

Be specific.

Instead of:

"Write product descriptions."

Say:

"Write 5 product descriptions for a handmade candle brand. Tone should feel warm, clean, and trustworthy. Each description should be

80 to 100 words. Focus on what the customer will enjoy about using the candle, not just the features. Avoid sounding cheesy or overly salesy."

That is a completely different instruction. And it will usually produce a much better starting point.

For almost any project, include these five things in your prompt:

- what you want created
- who it is for
- desired tone
- format or length
- what to avoid

Then ask for options.

Ask AI to give you three headline versions. Ask it to simplify a paragraph. Ask it to make a caption more natural. Ask it to tighten repetition. Ask it to sound less robotic.

You are directing the tool. You are not surrendering to it.

That mindset matters.

Step 5: Learn how to rescue mediocre AI output

This is one of the most profitable beginner skills you can build.

Because yes, sometimes AI gives you something flat, repetitive, awkward, or weirdly lifeless.

That does not mean you are stuck. It means the draft needs work.

Here is how to improve weak output quickly.

If it sounds generic, tell AI:
"Make this more specific and concrete."
"Remove clichés."
"Use plain English."
"Make this sound as if a real person wrote it."

If it sounds robotic, tell AI:
"Shorten the sentences."
"Make the tone more conversational."
"Reduce repetition."
"Remove formal-sounding phrases."

If it sounds weak, tell AI:
"Lead with the strongest benefit."
"Make this clearer and more persuasive."
"Tighten this so every sentence matters."

If the structure is messy, tell AI:
"Organise this into a cleaner format."
"Group similar ideas together."
"Turn this into a numbered or bullet-point structure."

Then do your own pass.

Read it out loud. This works better than silently scanning it.

When something sounds unnatural in your mouth, it usually sounds unnatural on the page too.

That one habit will catch a lot of bad phrasing.

Step 6: Run a quality check before you send anything

Never send work the second it is generated.

Pause and review it.

Before you deliver, ask yourself:

Did I solve the actual problem the client hired me for?
Is the information accurate?
Does this sound natural and clear?
Did I remove the obvious AI fluff?
Is the tone right for the audience?
Is the formatting clean?
Are there spelling, grammar, or naming errors?
Have I included everything I promised?

You do not need a forty-minute perfectionist ritual. You just need a final check that protects your reputation.

It is amazing how many problems can be prevented by ten focused minutes.

Step 7: Manage deadlines like someone people can trust

Clients are often more forgiving about imperfections than lateness.

If you say Friday, mean Friday.

Better yet, give yourself breathing room. If you think a task will take ninety minutes, do not promise it in ninety minutes unless you have to. Promise it later, then deliver early if possible.

This does two things:

It reduces your stress.

It increases the client's confidence in you.

Even a short check-in message helps.

Something like:

"Everything is on track. I'll have this over to you by 5 PM."

That makes people feel taken care of.

And if something does go wrong, do not disappear. Silence destroys trust much faster than honesty does.

A simple message works:

"I want to keep you updated. I need a little more time to make sure this is strong. I can send it by 7 PM instead of 5 PM."

Most reasonable clients can handle that. What they hate is chasing someone for answers.

Step 8: Know when to revise and when to stop

Revisions are part of the job. They are not proof that you failed.

Sometimes the client needs a tone change. Sometimes they want something slightly shorter. Sometimes you misunderstood a part of the brief. That is normal.

But do not let revision turn into endless, unpaid extra work.

Revise when:

- there is a real error

- the tone missed the mark
- the change is small and reasonable
- the request fits the original agreement

Push back politely when:

- the client keeps changing the goal
- they ask for extra deliverables
- they want multiple new versions beyond what was agreed
- they are treating one small job like unlimited access

A calm response might be:

"I'm happy to make one round of revisions based on the original brief. If you'd like a broader rewrite or additional versions, I can quote that separately."

That is not rude. That is business.

And the earlier you learn that, the easier this gets.

Step 9: Turn the first job into proof

The first payment matters. But the proof matters too.

Once the client is happy, do not just walk away.

Ask for one next step:

- a testimonial
- a referral
- permission to use the work as a sample

You can say:

"I'm really glad this helped. If you're happy with the result, would you be open to sending me a short testimonial I could use?"

Or:

"If you know anyone else who might need this kind of help, I'd really appreciate a referral."

Or:

"Would you be okay with me using this as an anonymised sample in my portfolio?"

This is how one small job becomes leverage.

And in the beginning, leverage matters almost as much as cash.

Practical Examples

Delivering a résumé upgrade package

Picture someone who has been applying for jobs for weeks with no response.

They are discouraged. They are tired of staring at the same résumé. They know it is weak, but they do not know how to fix it.

That person does not need magic. They need clarity.

So you ask for:

- their current résumé
- the kinds of jobs they want
- two or three job descriptions
- any achievements they do not want overlooked

Then you go to work.

You use AI to help rewrite bland bullet points into stronger ones. You improve the opening summary. You tailor language toward the roles they want. You clean up formatting so the document looks more polished and easier to scan.

But you do not blindly trust the draft.

You make sure the achievements sound believable. You remove exaggerated claims. You check that the wording still sounds like a real person with real experience.

Then you deliver:

- the updated résumé
- an editable version
- a clean final version
- a short note explaining what you improved

To that client, this is not "just writing."
It is a relief.
It is hope.
It is one less barrier between them and their next opportunity.

That is valuable.

Completing a social caption bundle in under 90 minutes

Now imagine a small-business owner with a decent product who never knows what to post.

They are busy. They are tired. They keep meaning to show up online, but the content keeps falling to the bottom of the list.

You offer a caption bundle.

You ask for:

- their website or offer
- who they sell to
- brand tone
- examples of posts they like
- any calls to action they want included

Then you build the batch in categories:

- educational captions
- promotional captions
- story or personal-style captions

AI helps you generate fast first drafts. Then you edit them so they actually sound like one brand instead of fifteen random internet posts.

You tighten the hooks. You remove repeated phrases. You make the call to action clearer. You label everything neatly.

Instead of dumping text into a doc, you deliver something organised and usable.

That is what makes the client feel they paid for a real service, not a rushed shortcut.

Writing product descriptions with a repeatable template

This is one of the easiest services to make efficient.

Say a seller has ten products and weak listings. The descriptions are bland, confusing, or too short. They know the products are good, but the writing is not helping them.

You do not need to reinvent your process for every item. Create a simple template.

A strong product description often follows this flow:

First, name the product and its main appeal.
Then highlight key features.
Then explain the practical benefit to the buyer.
Then end with a line that reinforces the experience or use case.

That structure speeds everything up.

You gather the basics for each product:

- name
- material or specs
- standout features
- ideal buyer
- practical use
- brand tone

AI helps you produce the first draft for each one. Then you edit so they do not all sound cloned. You vary phrasing. You make sure the details are accurate. You remove anything vague or over-the-top.

This is how you work faster as a beginner: not by rushing, but by using a repeatable structure.

Repurposing a YouTube video into short-form written content

This is a great beginner offer because the raw material already exists.

A creator has a video, but no time to turn it into posts, emails, or short-form content. They know there is value in the video, but it is trapped there.

You ask for:

- the video link
- transcript if available
- target platform
- audience
- preferred tone

Then you pull out the strongest ideas.

You use AI to summarise the video, extract main points, and generate possible posts. Then you step in and shape it. You choose the best angles. You remove filler. You make the content sound like the creator, not like a machine.

You might turn one video into:

- three LinkedIn posts
- five short-form posts
- one email

- ten future content ideas

To the client, that feels useful immediately. One piece of content becomes many.

That is not flashy work.
It is practical work.
And practical work gets bought every day.

Common Mistakes to Avoid

Relying on AI output without reviewing it

This one hurts beginners all the time.

The draft looks polished at first glance, so they assume it is ready. Then the client notices repetition, awkward phrasing, wrong details, or a tone that does not fit.

Never hand over raw AI output as if it were finished work.

Read it carefully.
Check facts.
Clean the language.
Make sure it actually sounds like something a human would say.

Your review is not optional. It is part of the service.

Missing deadlines because you got stuck overthinking

Overthinking feels responsible while you are doing it. But often, it is just fear wearing nicer clothes.

You keep adjusting, rewording, checking, and tweaking because sending the work feels vulnerable. Once you send it, it can be judged.

But late work creates a bigger problem than slightly imperfect work.

Do not let anxiety turn into delay.

Aim for strong and finished, not endlessly improved.

Sending messy files

Presentation matters more than people think.

A messy file name, poor formatting, random spacing, and a vague delivery message make the work feel cheaper. Even if the content is decent, the experience feels sloppy.

Clean up the document. Name the files properly. Label sections clearly. Make it easy to use.

Clients are not just reacting to what you made. They are reacting to how it feels to receive it.

Accepting vague requests without clarifying the goal

This is where trouble starts.

The client says, "I need help with my content," and you say yes too quickly because you do not want to lose the opportunity.

Now you are stuck trying to guess what "help" means.

Clarify the outcome before you begin.

What exactly do they need?
How much do they need?

Who is it for?

What should the finished result do?

A little clarity at the start can save you hours later.

Quick Win Task

Do this today, even if you do not have a client yet.

Pick one beginner-friendly service:

- résumé upgrade
- social caption bundle
- product descriptions
- video-to-content repurposing

Then complete this short exercise.

Write one sentence that defines success for the project.

List five questions you would ask the client before starting.

Create a raw material checklist.

Write one strong AI prompt for the service.

Make one sample deliverable using a fake business, your own background, or a public example.

Then review it using the quality checklist from this chapter.

That small exercise will teach you more than another three hours of scrolling, watching, or "learning."

Because the fastest way to stop feeling like a beginner is not to consume more information.

It is to practice delivering something real.

You do not need to become exceptional before you start earning.

You need to become reliable.

That may not sound glamorous, but it is powerful.

The internet is crowded with people trying to look impressive. Far fewer people know how to take a small problem, solve it well, and deliver without complicating things.

Be that person.

Be the person who asks good questions.
Who pays attention?
Who improves the rough draft?
Who sends clean work?
Who meets the deadline?
Who makes the client feel relieved they hired you?

That is how trust is built.

And trust is what creates repeat work, referrals, testimonials, and confidence.

Your first few jobs may not be perfect. That is fine. They do not need to be.

They need to be honest, useful, and finished.

That is enough to get moving.

And when you are struggling financially, movement matters.

One delivered result can change the way you see yourself. It stops being a theory. It stops being "maybe someday." It becomes proof that you can solve a problem and get paid for it.

That is a big shift.

So do not wait to feel fully ready.
Do not wait until you sound like an expert.
Do not wait until the fear disappears.

Take the work seriously. Do it carefully. Deliver it cleanly.

That is how beginners become professionals.

Not all at once.

One finished job at a time.

Chapter 9: The Fastest Beginner AI Income Methods: Choose One and Execute

When money feels tight, too much advice becomes its own kind of stress.

One person tells you to start a digital product. Another says freelance. Someone else says build an audience first, grow a newsletter, learn automation, study prompts, pick a niche, make content, and post every day.

Meanwhile, your actual problem is much simpler.

You need money.

Not theory. Not another ten-hour rabbit hole. Not a spreadsheet full of ideas you never act on. You need a method that makes sense, one offer you can put in front of real people, and a clear way to get from zero to your first payment.

That is what this chapter is about.

You do not need six income methods. You need one that fits your situation well enough to start. That is how beginners get traction. Not by chasing every opportunity, but by picking one practical lane and staying in it long enough to get results.

If you have been circling ideas and still have nothing to show for it, this chapter is your reset button.

By the end, you will know which beginner-friendly AI income method to choose, how to offer it, how to deliver it, where to find clients, and what to do today to get moving.

Reality Check

Before we go further, let's clear something up.

AI can help you work faster. It can help you brainstorm, draft, organise, rewrite, simplify, and structure. It can save you time. It can help you produce useful work sooner than you could on your own.

What it cannot do is build trust for you.

It cannot care about a client's goal. It cannot notice when the tone feels off. It cannot spot every mistake. It cannot ask a smart follow-up question at the right moment. It cannot replace judgment.

That matters because beginners often get stuck in one of two extremes.

The first extreme is fear:
"I don't know enough yet. I'm not qualified. I need more time."

The second extreme is fantasy:
"AI will do everything. I'll just copy, paste, and get paid."

Neither one works.

The truth lives in the middle.

You do not need to be an expert. But you do need to be useful.

That is the whole game.

Useful to the stressed job seeker who cannot turn their work history into a strong résumé.
Useful to the bakery owner who has photos to post but no captions.
Useful to the Etsy seller with weak product descriptions.
Useful to the coach, sitting on a goldmine of long-form content they never repurpose.
Useful to the consultant drowning in admin and research tasks.

That is why the fastest beginner income methods are not glamorous. They are practical. They solve obvious problems. They save someone time, effort, or mental energy. And because the value is easy to understand, they are much easier to sell.

You are not trying to look impressive here. You are trying to become helpful enough that someone says, "Yes, that would make my life easier."

That is the standard.

And that standard is far more reachable than most people think.

Solution Breakdown

There are dozens of ways to use AI to make money. Most are too broad, too slow, or too dependent on building an audience first. For a beginner, the best options have three things in common:

They solve a real problem.

They can be delivered with basic tools.

They can lead to income quickly.

Here are six of the strongest beginner-friendly methods.

Method 1: AI-Assisted Résumé and Cover Letter Service

Who needs it

People who are job hunting are often overwhelmed, discouraged, and tired of trying to "sell themselves" on paper.

They know they have done real work. They know they have value. But when it is time to write a résumé or cover letter, everything turns vague. Their experience gets flattened into dull bullet points. Their achievements sound smaller than they are. Their confidence drops before they even hit apply.

That is where this service becomes valuable.

Your clients might be:

- Someone applying after a layoff
- A parent returning to work after a long gap
- A graduate with little experience and no idea how to present themselves
- A worker trying to move into a better-paying role
- A career changer who needs help translating old experience into a new direction

This is a strong beginner offer because the pain is clear. People do not enjoy doing this work themselves, and the need feels urgent.

What to offer

Keep your offer narrow and useful.

Do not position yourself as a "career transformation expert." You do not need that. You are offering support with specific documents that help someone apply with more confidence.

You could offer:

- Résumé rewrite
- Cover letter rewrite
- LinkedIn summary rewrite
- A bundled "job application refresh"

A simple package might be:

Basic
One résumé rewrite with stronger bullet points and cleaner wording

Standard
One résumé rewrite plus one tailored cover letter

Premium
Résumé, cover letter, and LinkedIn summary refresh

This is enough. Clear offers are easier to buy than vague promises.

How to deliver

Ask for:

- Their current résumé

- A target job title

- One or two example job listings

- Any extra context about what they actually did in past roles

Then do the work in a simple sequence.

First, read the résumé carefully. Look for vague phrases, weak bullet points, poor structure, and missing accomplishments.

Second, use AI to help rewrite the content. Ask it to turn flat job duties into clear, results-focused bullet points. Ask it for stronger summary options. Ask for multiple versions so you can choose the best one.

Third, edit it like a real person. This part matters more than most beginners realise. AI loves generic phrases. "Results-driven professional." "Dynamic team player." "Proven track record." These sound polished, but they say almost nothing. Cut them. Replace them with language that feels grounded and specific.

Fourth, tailor the cover letter to the role. Not with fake passion. With relevance. Show that the candidate understands the role and can speak to it clearly.

Fifth, deliver it neatly. One clean file. No clutter. No messy notes. No confusing versions.

Where to find clients

You do not need a huge platform for this.

Start with people who already know someone looking for work:

- Friends
- Family
- Former co-workers
- Local community groups
- Facebook groups
- LinkedIn connections
- University or college alumni groups
- Job seeker communities

You can also reach out to people who have publicly mentioned job searching or layoffs.

A message like this works:

"Hi, I saw that you're applying for new roles. I help people improve their résumés and cover letters so they come across more clearly and confidently. I'd be happy to show you a sample before you decide."

That last line lowers pressure. It gives the other person room to respond without feeling cornered.

Income example: 10 clients at $75–$100

This is one of the easiest ways to understand the path to your first $1,000.

Ten clients at $75 is $750.
Ten clients at $100 is $1,000.

That is not a fantasy number. It is a small, concrete service sold to people with a real need.

You do not need hundreds of customers. You need a handful of yeses.

And because job seekers talk to each other, one good experience can lead to referrals faster than you might expect.

Method 2: Social Media Caption Packs for Small Businesses

What businesses need most?

Most small business owners do not need more ideas. They need help turning ideas into posts they can actually use.

They are busy running the business, replying to customers, handling stock, doing appointments, chasing payments, fixing problems, and trying to keep everything moving. Social media usually gets pushed to the side until late at night, when they are too tired to think clearly.

That is why so many business pages look abandoned, inconsistent, or rushed.

This is your opportunity.

A small business does not need a "full-stack content ecosystem." It needs someone who can make posting easier.

That means:

- Captions that sound natural

- Promotional posts that do not feel desperate

- Seasonal content ideas

- Trust-building posts

- Simple calls to action

Businesses like these often need help:

- Salons

- Coaches

- Gyms

- Real estate agents

- Photographers

- Cafés

- Therapists

- Local service businesses

- Online shops

Monthly or one-off packages

You can offer this in two ways.

The first is a one-off caption pack:

- 12 captions

- 15 captions

- 20 captions

This is a great entry offer because it is simple and easy to understand.

The second is a monthly service:

- A set number of captions each month

- Optional content ideas
- Optional post themes
- Optional scheduling notes

Monthly work is attractive because the client's needs repeat. Every month, they need fresh content. That means one sale can become recurring income instead of a one-time payment.

How to deliver

Ask the client for:

- Their website or social media page
- Their services or products
- Their tone of voice
- Their ideal customer
- Any offers or promotions coming up
- Past posts they liked or that performed well

Then use AI to generate ideas and caption drafts. But do not stop there.

This is where mediocre work becomes good work.

A generic caption pack says:

"Treat yourself today."

"Book now."

"We love our clients."

That is filler.

A better caption pack reflects the actual business:

- The bakery's Saturday rush
- The salon's popular treatment
- The estate agent's local market knowledge
- The gym's beginner-friendly energy
- The photographer's style and process

The closer the captions feel to the business, the more valuable your work becomes.

Deliver everything in a simple document or spreadsheet with clear headings:

- Post idea
- Caption
- Suggested image or angle
- Call to action

Now the client is not just receiving words. They are receiving relief.

Income example: 5 clients at $150–$200

Five clients at $150 is $750.
Five clients at $200 is $1,000.

That is what makes this method powerful. You do not need to chase tiny gigs. A small number of decent clients can get you to your goal.

And once you have one business niche working well, the next one gets easier. If you have already created captions for one café, the second café will take less mental effort. If you have done good work for a yoga teacher, another wellness client becomes easier to serve.

That is how momentum starts.

Method 3: Product Descriptions for Etsy, eBay, and Shopify Sellers

Fast turnaround offer

This is one of the most underrated beginner services.

Most sellers are focused on products, orders, and customer questions. They do not want to sit there writing twenty product descriptions. So they either rush the job, copy the same wording everywhere, or leave the listings dull and incomplete.

That hurts sales.

A good description does not need to sound fancy. It needs to help the customer understand the product quickly and feel more confident buying it.

You can offer:

- Ten product descriptions rewritten
- Twenty listings improved
- Product titles, bullet points, and descriptions
- Etsy listing refreshes
- Shopify product page rewrites
- eBay listing clean-up

This is especially useful for:

- Handmade sellers

- Vintage sellers
- Small e-commerce brands
- People with lots of listings
- Sellers whose products are better than their copy

How to deliver

Ask for:

- Product links or photos
- Existing descriptions
- Key details like materials, sizes, colours, use cases, and shipping notes
- Brand tone
- Any keywords they want to include

Then build each listing around a simple goal: make the product easier to understand and easier to want.

AI can help you brainstorm features, benefits, structure, and phrasing. But your job is to make the final wording feel real.

Weak listing copy sounds like this:
"Beautiful handmade candle for any home."

That could describe almost anything.

Stronger copy sounds like this:
"Hand-poured soy candle with a warm vanilla scent, designed for cosy evenings, gifting, or adding a soft, calming feel to your space."

That gives the buyer something to picture.

When you work on product descriptions, clarity matters more than cleverness. A buyer should understand the item fast. They should know what it is, who it is for, and why it is worth buying.

Income example: 4 clients at $200–$250

Four clients at $200 is $800.
Four clients at $250 is $1,000.

Because sellers often need batches of listings done at once, this method can get you to your income goal with fewer clients.

That is a big advantage if you would rather do deeper work for a smaller number of people.

Method 4: Content Repurposing for Creators and Coaches

Turning long content into posts, captions, summaries, and emails

This is one of the smartest offers in this chapter because it solves a problem that many creators and coaches feel every single week.

They have content. In fact, they often have too much of it.

They have long podcast episodes, video recordings, webinars, live streams, newsletters, workshop notes, and voice notes full of ideas. But that content is trapped in long form. It never gets turned into short posts, emails, summaries, or social content.

So they keep creating more, while the old content sits unused.

That is wasted value.

Your job is to unlock it.

You take one long piece of content and turn it into several smaller assets:

- Social posts
- Captions
- Email drafts
- Summaries
- Quote ideas
- Content snippets
- Short-form post angles

This is deeply valuable because you are not asking the client to create more. You are helping them get more from what they already have.

How to deliver

Ask for:

- The original content link, transcript, notes, or recording
- Their audience
- Their preferred platforms
- Their tone of voice
- Their main message or offer
- Past content examples, if available

Then build a deliverable around practical outputs.

For example:

- 5 LinkedIn posts

- 8 Instagram captions

- 1 newsletter draft

- 1 content summary

- 3 quote-card text options

The key is not to "chop up" the original content lazily. Your work should feel shaped, not sliced.

That means:

- Pulling out strong ideas

- Making each piece stand on its own

- Keeping the creator's voice where possible

- Removing repetition and filler

- Structuring each asset for its platform

A coach talking about confidence should not receive ten watered-down versions of the same sentence. They should receive clear, useful pieces that sound like them and move the audience in a meaningful way.

Income example: 4 clients at $250

Four clients at $250 is $1,000.

That is what makes this offer so attractive. You can reach the goal with relatively few clients, and the work often turns into repeat business because creators keep producing content.

If the first batch helps them save time and stay visible online, they often want another batch next week or next month.

Method 5: Simple Digital Templates and Printable Products

What to create

This method is less about custom client work and more about creating something once and selling it multiple times.

Examples include:

- Budget planners
- Habit trackers
- Goal-setting worksheets
- Meal planners
- Study planners
- Small business checklists
- Client onboarding templates
- Content calendars
- Printable journals
- Canva templates
- Notion templates

This works best when the product is clear, useful, and easy to understand.

Most beginners make the mistake of trying to create something elaborate. But simple often sells better than complicated. A clean weekly planner that solves one frustration is more useful than a fifty-page "life system" nobody finishes.

How to use AI for research, text, and structure

AI is helpful here in a different way.

It can help you:

- Find common pain points in a niche
- Generate product ideas
- Organise a template logically
- Draft prompts, sections, instructions, or worksheet questions
- Improve titles and descriptions
- Create variations of the same concept

Let's say you want to make a simple content planner for busy small business owners. AI can help you structure sections like:

- Weekly content goals
- Post ideas
- Offer reminders
- Promotions
- Engagement prompts
- Content notes

Then you take that structure and turn it into a clean design in Canva or another simple tool.

When this method works best

This method works best when:

- You want less direct client interaction
- You enjoy organizing ideas into useful resources
- You are comfortable testing and improving products
- You can be patient while listings gain traction

This is important: for most beginners, this is not the fastest cash method.

It can absolutely work. But it often takes more time upfront. You have to create the product, design it, list it, describe it, and wait for sales. If you need money urgently, a service is usually the better first move.

Think of digital products as a quieter, slower-growing path. A good one. But usually not the fastest first one.

Method 6: Research and Admin Support with AI

Lead lists, summaries, email drafts, and idea generation

Some people are not excited by writing social posts or rewriting résumés. They are better at organizing information, summarizing, sorting, and helping busy people stay on top of small but important tasks.

If that sounds like you, this method may fit you better than the others.

A lot of founders, consultants, coaches, recruiters, and small business owners are constantly behind on tasks like:

- Researching leads
- Summarising articles or calls
- Drafting emails
- Collecting competitor information
- Brainstorming ideas
- Organising notes
- Preparing rough first drafts

These tasks drain time and attention. And because they are repetitive, people are often happy to pay for help.

Best clients for this offer

Look for people who are busy, a bit stretched, and doing too much themselves:

- Solo consultants
- Coaches
- Recruiters
- Sales professionals
- Agencies
- Small business owners
- Online service providers
- Start-up founders

They may not need a full-time assistant. But they often need someone dependable who can take care of a specific set of tasks each week.

You can offer:

- Lead list building

- Research packs

- Meeting summaries

- Draft email support

- Weekly admin bundles

- Idea generation and organisation

How to deliver

Because this work often involves information, accuracy matters.

Double-check names. Double-check links. Double-check facts. Do not assume AI got it right.

A simple offer might look like this:

- Fifty qualified leads in a spreadsheet

- Ten draft outreach emails

- Five article summaries

- Twenty content ideas

- Delivered within a clear timeframe

This service is especially strong if you are detail-oriented and reliable. Clients will forgive beginner branding much faster than they will forgive careless work.

If you become the person who does what they said they would do, on time, in a clean format, you instantly become more valuable.

Decision Guide

Now let's make this easier.

You do not need the best method in some abstract sense. You need the best method for your current reality.

Best method for fastest cash

AI-assisted résumé and cover letter service

or

Product descriptions for Etsy, eBay, and Shopify sellers

Why these two?

Because the pain is immediate, people either need a better application now or they need better listings now. The value is easy to explain, and the sale does not require a long education process.

If you need money sooner rather than later, start with urgency.

Best method for the least writing

Research and admin support with AI

There is still some writing involved, but less persuasive writing. This is a better fit if you prefer structure, organisation, and summaries over creative copy.

Best method for the least client interaction

Simple digital templates and printable products

You create the product once, list it, and sell it without custom conversations for every sale. This is better if you like independence and dislike back-and-forth communication.

Just remember: less interaction usually means slower results at first.

Best method for a repeat monthly income

Social media caption packs

or

Content repurposing for creators and coaches

These naturally lend themselves to recurring work. Businesses need regular content. Creators keep producing long-form material. Once a client sees the value, it is easy for them to hire you again.

If your goal is stability, these are strong choices.

Step-by-Step Action Plan

Now it is time to stop thinking in circles and move.

Here is the plan.

Step 1: Choose one method today

Not tomorrow. Today.

Do not choose based on what sounds the most exciting in theory. Choose based on what feels the easiest to start with, the skills and energy you have right now.

Ask yourself:

- Do I like writing?
- Do I prefer organising information?
- Do I want quick cash or slower long-term income?
- Do I mind client communication?
- Which type of person would I feel most comfortable helping?

Then pick one method and commit to it for the next two weeks.

Not forever. Just long enough to give it a fair chance.

Step 2: Write your offer in one sentence

Use this structure:

"I help [type of person] get [result] by delivering [specific service]."

Examples:

- I help job seekers improve their applications by rewriting résumés and cover letters.
- I help small businesses stay consistent online by creating ready-to-post caption packs.
- I help Etsy and Shopify sellers improve their listings with clearer, more persuasive product descriptions.
- I help creators turn long-form content into short-form posts, summaries, and email drafts.
- I help busy founders with AI-assisted research, lead lists, and admin support.

This sentence gives you clarity fast.

Step 3: Create one sample

You do not need a huge portfolio. You need one piece of proof.

Make one simple sample based on the method you chose:

- Rewrite part of a résumé
- Create five sample captions for a business

- Rewrite three product descriptions
- Turn one video transcript into several posts
- Build one printable page
- Create a sample lead spreadsheet

The point is not perfection. The point is to show someone what your work looks like.

Step 4: Set a beginner-friendly price

You are not trying to charge premium rates on day one. You are trying to make it easy for someone to say yes.

Examples:

- Résumé package: $75–$100
- Caption pack: $150–$200
- Product description batch: $200–$250
- Repurposing package: $250
- Admin or research package: $100–$250 depending on scope

Your first goal is proof, not prestige.

Step 5: Find ten realistic prospects

This matters more than your logo, your website, or your bio.

Find ten people or businesses who could genuinely use your help.

For example:

- Ten job seekers
- Ten small businesses with weak or inconsistent social media

- Ten Etsy sellers with poor listings
- Ten creators with long videos but almost no repurposed content
- Ten consultants or founders who look overloaded

Write down their names. Make it real.

Step 6: Send outreach messages

This is the moment most beginners avoid.

Do it anyway.

Keep the message short and based on what you noticed.

Examples:

"Hi, I came across your page and noticed you've got great visuals but inconsistent captions. I help small businesses by creating ready-to-post caption packs that save time and make posting easier. Happy to send a short sample if useful."

"Hi, I saw your Etsy listings and noticed a few descriptions could be clearer and more benefit-focused. I help sellers improve listings with faster, cleaner product copy. If helpful, I can send a quick sample rewrite."

"Hi, I noticed you're applying for new roles. I help job seekers improve their résumés and cover letters so they sound stronger and more targeted. I'd be happy to show you a short sample."

Do not try to sound overly clever. Sounds helpful.

Step 7: Deliver quickly and cleanly

When someone says yes, keep things simple.

Confirm:

- What they need
- What is included
- When will you deliver
- What materials do you need from them

Then do the work.

And before you send it, review everything carefully. Fix awkward wording. Remove generic phrases. Check for mistakes. Make sure the final result feels polished and easy to use.

People will remember that you made their lives easier.

Step 8: Turn one job into the next one

After you deliver, do not vanish.

Ask:

- Did this help?
- Would you like another batch next week or next month?
- Would you be open to a short testimonial?
- Do you know anyone else who might need this?

This is how a one-off job becomes momentum.

Not with tricks. With good work and a clear next step.

Common Mistakes to Avoid

Trying to do all six methods at once

This is the fastest way to stay broke while feeling busy.

Pick one lane. Learn it. Improve it. Let it pay you before you expand.

Spending days "getting ready"

A lot of beginners hide in preparation because it feels productive.

They tweak their offer. Redesign the sample. Rename the package. Rewrite the bio. Watch more videos. Read more threads.

None of that matters if nobody sees the offer.

At some point, preparation turns into avoidance.

Sending generic AI output

Clients can feel when something is flat, vague, or soulless.

If the work sounds like it could apply to anyone, it is not ready to send. You must add specificity, tone, and context. That is the difference between "AI-generated" and "genuinely useful."

Making the offer too broad

Do not promise everything.

A beginner's offer should be narrow, clear, and easy to deliver. The more vague your service becomes, the harder it is to explain, sell, and complete.

Being sloppy with delivery

Messy files, missed deadlines, bad formatting, unclear communication, and avoidable mistakes will damage trust quickly.

You do not need to look like a giant agency. But you do need to look dependable.

Taking silence personally

Not everyone will reply. Not everyone will be interested. That is normal.

A few ignored messages do not mean the method is broken. They mean you are doing outreach, which is part of how business works.

Do not let silence talk you out of something that still has real potential.

Quick Win Task

Here is what to do before today ends.

Pick one of the six methods.

Then do these five things:

1. Write your one-sentence offer
2. Make one sample
3. Choose one price
4. List ten potential clients or prospects
5. Send three outreach messages

That is it.

Not build a brand.

Not overthink your niche.

Not consume another three hours of content.

Just do the work that creates a chance of getting paid.

That is the shift.

You do not need a perfect business model right now.

You need a starting point that works.

Your first $1,000 is rarely about genius. It is usually about courage, consistency, and usefulness. It is about choosing a simple offer, putting it in front of real people, and being willing to improve as you go.

The first few steps may feel uncomfortable. You may worry that you are too new, too late, too unqualified, too awkward, too far behind.

You are not.

You are just at the beginning.

And beginnings are supposed to feel clumsy.

What matters is not whether you feel fully ready. What matters is whether you act before confidence arrives. Because confidence usually shows up after motion, not before it.

So choose your method.

Make the sample.

Send the messages.

Let real-world response teach you what to improve.

That is how this stops being an interesting idea and starts becoming income.

That is how a beginner becomes someone who has made money with AI.

And once you do it once, even in a small way, everything changes.

Chapter 10: Make the First $1,000 Inevitable: Numbers, Targets, and Daily Execution

When you are stressed about money, vague effort feels strangely comforting.

It lets you say, "I'm working on it," without facing the harder question: *Am I doing the kind of work that actually leads to getting paid?*

A lot of people spend their first week trying to make money with AI, doing things that feel productive but do not move the needle. They watch tutorials. Test tools. Rewrite their bio. Change their offer three times. Make a logo that no client asked for. Organise folders. Take notes. Think very hard.

At the end of the week, they are exhausted.

And still broke.

That is not because they are lazy. It is because unclear work creates unclear results.

If you are reading this while worried about rent, bills, debt, groceries, or just the embarrassment of checking your bank balance too often, I want to say something plainly: you do not need more hype. You do not need a perfect plan. You do not need to become an expert by next Tuesday.

You need a simple target, clear numbers, and a daily system that keeps you moving even when your emotions are all over the place.

That is how the first $1,000 stops feeling like a dream and starts becoming a series of doable steps.

Not easy. Not instant. But doable.

Reality Check

The first $1,000 usually does not come from brilliance.

It comes from repetition.

From sending the message, you do not feel like sending.
From following up when it would be easier to assume they are not interested.
From sticking with one offer long enough to learn what people respond to.
From tracking what is happening instead of relying on memory, mood, or wishful thinking.

This is the part many beginners get wrong.

They set a money goal, but they do not build a behaviour plan underneath it.

So they say things like:

"I want to make $1,000 this month."

Fine. But how?

How many people will you contact?

How many follow-ups will you send?

How many conversations do you need?

How many offers will you make?

What price are you charging?

How will you know if the plan is working?

Without answers to those questions, the goal is just pressure in a nicer outfit.

And pressure alone is not a strategy.

Here is the truth that calms people down once they really understand it:

Your first $1,000 is not one giant leap. It is a small stack of clear sales.

That is good news.

Because "make $1,000" sounds heavy.
But "sell five $200 offers" sounds possible.
"Sell ten $100 offers" sounds even more possible.

The moment you break the goal into numbers, your brain stops treating it like a foggy fantasy and starts seeing it as a path.

That shift matters more than most people realise.

Solution Breakdown

Why vague effort creates vague results

If your daily plan is "try to get clients," you will almost always underperform.

That kind of goal is too slippery. You can spend three hours "trying" and still avoid the hard parts.

A clear plan sounds different.

It sounds like:

- send 15 outreach messages
- follow up with 5 old leads
- improve one sample
- ask for the sale in at least 2 conversations
- log every action in a tracker

Now you know what done looks like.

That matters because when money is tight, emotions distort everything. One quiet day can make you feel like nothing is working. One nice reply can make you think success is around the corner. Both can mislead you.

Numbers keep you honest.

They show you whether you are truly in the game or just hovering around it.

A beginner named Marcus learned this the hard way. He kept saying he was "building an AI side hustle," but for ten days, he mostly researched tools, watched tutorials, and rewrote his service description. He felt busy, even proud of how much he was learning. But he had only contacted six people.

Six.

Once he finally admitted that to himself, everything changed. He picked one offer, set a daily outreach goal, and stopped judging progress by how motivated he felt. Two weeks later, he had his first paying client.

Not because he discovered a secret.

Because he replaced vague effort with measurable action.

The math behind the first $1,000

A thousand dollars feels intimidating when you look at it as one big number. It feels lighter when you slice it into smaller wins.

Here are four realistic ways to get there.

10 sales at $100

This is one of the easiest starting models for beginners.

You are offering something small, useful, and easy to say yes to. For example:

- résumé and cover letter rewrites
- product description bundles
- social media caption packs
- simple research summaries
- basic customer FAQ writing

Ten people paying $100 each gives you $1,000.

This model works well when you want a low-friction offer that feels approachable to buyers and manageable for you to deliver.

5 sales at $200

This is often the sweet spot.

The offer is still small enough to sell without requiring much trust, but large enough that you do not need a long list of clients.

Examples:

- 30 social media captions for a small business
- a résumé, cover letter, and LinkedIn rewrite
- optimised product descriptions for a set number of items
- a welcome email sequence for a small creator or coach

Five sales. That is it.

For many people, this is the cleanest route to the first $1,000.

4 sales at $250

At this point, the offer should feel more complete and outcome-driven.

Examples:

- a personal branding package for job seekers
- a one-month content support package
- a listing optimisation package for online sellers
- a customer response template pack for small service businesses

Four buyers are not a lot. But the offer needs to feel solid, specific, and worth the price.

2 sales at $500

This is possible, but it is usually better once you have a little confidence and at least a tiny bit of proof.

A $500 offer can work if it solves a clear business problem and saves the client time or helps them make money faster. But for a total beginner, it is often harder to sell because the buyer needs more trust before saying yes.

That does not mean you cannot do it. It just means you should be honest about what is easiest to sell first.

Building a beginner-friendly income target

Your target should challenge you, but it should also make sense for where you are right now.

This is where beginners often sabotage themselves. They create a plan that sounds impressive, rather than one they can actually execute.

A beginner-friendly target has three qualities.

First, it is simple to explain. You should be able to describe your offer in one sentence without sounding confused.

Second, it is easy to track. You should know exactly how many sales you need.

Third, it is realistic to deliver. You should not be creating an offer so complicated that one client drains your whole week.

For most beginners, the best starting targets are:

- 10 sales at $100
- 5 sales at $200

Those are not tiny goals. They are focused goals.

And focused goals build momentum.

Activity goals vs result goals

This distinction can save you a lot of unnecessary self-doubt.

A result goal is what you want:

- make $1,000
- get 5 clients
- close 10 sales

A result goal matters. But you do not fully control it.

An activity goal is what you do:

- send 15 messages today
- follow up with 5 people
- create a better sample
- ask two warm contacts for referrals
- make three direct offers this week

You control those.

That is why activity goals matter so much, especially in the beginning. They give you something to win each day before the money shows up.

If you only judge yourself by money, the first quiet week can crush you.
If you judge yourself by actions, you can still build momentum while the results catch up.

That is not just practical. It is emotionally protective.

Because when someone is already financially stressed, they do not need a system that makes them feel like a failure every night. They need a system that says, *you did the right work today. Keep going.*

The daily scoreboard that keeps you moving

You need a scoreboard because your feelings are unreliable.

On hard days, you will think you have done more than you actually have.
On discouraged days, you will think you have done nothing.
Both are dangerous.

A scoreboard gives you the truth.

Keep it simple. Track these numbers every day:

- new outreach messages sent
- follow-ups sent
- replies received
- conversations started

- offers made
- payments received

That is enough.

This small habit changes your decision-making. It helps you see where the real problem is.

For example:

- If you are sending messages but getting no replies, the message or audience needs work.
- If people reply but conversations go nowhere, your pitch may be too vague.
- If conversations happen but nobody buys, your offer may be unclear, under-explained, or priced awkwardly.
- If people seem interested but then disappear, you may not be following up properly.

Without a scoreboard, you guess.
With a scoreboard, you adjust.

How many outreach messages, samples, and follow-ups to aim for

You do not need perfect numbers. You need useful numbers.

A strong beginner baseline looks like this:

Each weekday:

- 10 to 20 new outreach messages
- 5 to 10 follow-ups

- 1 improvement to your offer, message, or sample

Each week:

- 1 to 3 relevant samples
- 5 to 10 real conversations
- 3 to 5 direct offers made

That might sound like a lot at first, but remember: this is not eight hours of hard labour. Much of it can be done in short sessions.

A person working evenings could do:

- 20 minutes of outreach in the morning
- 15 minutes of follow-ups at lunch
- 30 to 45 minutes at night for conversations, samples, or delivery

Across four weeks, those numbers add up.

Let's say you send 250-300 messages a month.

That could realistically lead to:

- 25 to 40 replies
- 15 to 20 genuine conversations
- 8 to 12 offers
- 5 sales at $200

There is your $1,000.

Not guaranteed, of course. Real life is messier than neat math. But this is the kind of volume that gives you a real shot instead of a hopeful one.

How to stay consistent when results are slow

This is where most people wobble.

Not at the beginning, when everything feels fresh.
Not after the first sale, when hope returns.

They wobble in the middle.

After a few days of effort.
Before obvious results.
When the excitement wears off, silence starts to feel personal.

That is the dangerous stretch.

A woman I'll call Lena started offering AI-assisted résumé help after getting laid off. She needed money quickly and was scared to waste time. In her first week, she messaged people, polished samples, and posted in a few groups. Almost nothing happened.

She told herself the market was too crowded.
Then she told herself she was bad at selling.
Then she started thinking maybe she should switch to a different offer altogether.

But when she reviewed her numbers, she saw something important: she had sent only 28 messages, followed up with almost no one, and her pitch focused on "AI optimisation" rather than what people actually cared about getting interviews faster and feeling more confident when applying.

So she did not quit.

She simplified.

She followed up.

She kept the same offer.

A few days later, she landed her first client.

That is what staying consistent looks like in real life. It is not glamorous. It often feels awkward and repetitive. But consistency is what lets your small improvements compound.

When results are slow, remind yourself of this:
Silence is not always rejection.
Sometimes it is just a thin pipeline.

What to do if the first offer gets no response

If nobody responds, do not immediately assume the whole business idea is dead.

Look at the three most common causes.

1. The audience is wrong

Your offer may be fine, but you are showing it to people who do not urgently need it.

For example, résumé help should go to active job seekers, not random professionals. Product description help should go to sellers with weak listings, not just anyone who owns an online store.

2. The positioning is weak

If your message sounds abstract, clever, or overly technical, people will ignore it.

Compare these two approaches:

"I provide AI-powered content optimisation services."

Versus:

"I can rewrite your Etsy product descriptions so they sound clearer, more persuasive, and easier for buyers to trust."

The second one is easier to understand and easier to buy.

3. The offer feels too big or too risky

If people do not know you, a big offer with a high price can feel like too much.

Sometimes the fix is not lowering the price. Sometimes it is shrinking the scope.

Instead of offering "full content strategy," offer "15 custom captions for one month of posts."
Instead of "career branding optimisation," offer "résumé and cover letter rewrite."

Clear and contained often beats broad and impressive.

When to adjust pricing, positioning, or audience

The key is not to change everything at once.

That is what panicked beginners do. They rewrite the offer, lower the price, switch niches, and create a new sample all in the same afternoon. Then they have no idea what actually helped.

Change one thing. Measure. Then decide.

Here is a practical way to diagnose it.

Adjust the positioning if:

- People read the message but do not reply
- They seem confused about what you are offering
- Your wording focuses more on process than result

Adjust the audience if:

- The people you contact do not have the problem urgently enough
- You are pitching too broadly
- Your offer makes sense, but not for the people seeing it

Adjust the price if:

- People are interested but hesitate at the final step
- You are having real conversations, but nobody commits
- The offer is still a bit too large for the trust you have built

A good rule: give an offer enough reps before judging it.

If you have sent fewer than 50 targeted messages, it is usually too early to declare failure.

If you have had several conversations and still have no closure, now you have useful feedback.

If you have delivered one or two jobs successfully, you can now start improving the packaging and maybe raise the price.

Patience matters.

But measured patience matters more.

Step-by-Step Action Plan

Here is how to make this chapter practical.

Step 1: Choose your first $1,000 model

Pick one path:

- 10 sales at $100
- 5 sales at $200
- 4 sales at $250
- 2 sales at $500

If you are brand new, choose either 10 at $100 or 5 at $200.

Do not spend three days debating. Pick the version that feels clear enough to act on now.

Write it down in one sentence:

"My goal is 5 sales at $200 for AI-assisted social media caption packs."

Or:

"My goal is 10 sales at $100 for résumé and cover letter rewrites."

Now you have something concrete.

Step 2: Choose one offer and one audience

Not three offers.

Not "anyone who needs help."

One offer. One audience.

Examples:

- résumé rewrites for job seekers
- caption packs for local businesses
- product descriptions for Etsy sellers
- simple email writing for coaches or creators
- FAQ and customer response templates for service businesses

Then write your offer like a normal person would say it.

Bad version:

"I offer AI-driven copy support for digital-first brands."

Better version:

"I help small businesses by writing ready-to-post social captions so they can stay visible online without staring at a blank screen."

If it sounds like marketing fluff, simplify it again.

Step 3: Build a simple tracker

Open a spreadsheet or notebook and make these columns:

- date
- person or business name
- where you found them
- what you offered
- outreach sent
- reply
- follow-up sent
- conversation happened

- offer made

- outcome

- amount

- paid

This takes ten minutes to set up and can save you weeks of confusion.

Without a tracker, you will forget who you contacted, miss easy follow-ups, and make decisions based on emotion.

With a tracker, patterns become obvious.

Step 4: Set daily action targets

Use this as your starting point:

- 15 new messages a day
- 5 follow-ups a day
- 1 sample improvement or message improvement a day

That is enough to create momentum without becoming overwhelming.

And yes, it can be done even if your schedule is packed.

What matters is not whether you do it in one long block. What matters is whether it gets done.

Step 5: Use a daily scoreboard

At the end of every day, write down:

- messages sent

- follow-ups sent

- replies received

- conversations started

- offers made

- sales closed

- money collected

This gives you a daily reality check.

You may not have a sale today. But if you hit your action targets, the day still counts. That is how you avoid the trap of thinking "nothing happened" just because no money came in before dinner.

Step 6: Review the week like a business owner

Once a week, sit down and review your numbers.

Ask:

- How many people did I reach out to?

- How many replied?

- How many conversations turned into real interest?

- How many offers did I make?

- Where am I losing momentum?

- What is one thing I can improve next week?

Do not use this review session to shame yourself.

Use it to learn.

That is how professionals improve. They do not rely on random bursts of energy. They look at what happened and make better decisions.

Step 7: Use the "stuck? Do this next" checklist

Whenever you feel frozen, do one of these:

- send 5 new messages
- follow up with every unanswered lead from two days ago
- rewrite your offer in simpler words
- create a better sample
- ask one warm contact if they know someone who needs your help
- review your last 10 messages and make them less wordy
- make your call to action clearer
- reduce the scope of the offer so it feels easier to buy
- post your offer in one relevant online community

The cure for feeling stuck is usually not more thinking.

It is one clean action.

What to do today

Do these five things before the day ends:

1. Pick your income path
   Choose: 10 at $100 or 5 at $200.
2. Write your offer in one sentence
   Keep it plain and specific.

3. Create your tracker

    nothing fancy. Just usable.

4. Send 10 targeted outreach messages

    not random messages. Targeted ones.

5. Follow up with 3 people, or create 1 strong sample if you have

    no leads yet

    either move existing opportunities forward or create proof that

    helps you start conversations.

If you do those five things today, you are no longer "thinking about starting."

You have started.

Common Mistakes to Avoid

Measuring success only by money in the first week

This is one of the fastest ways to burn out.

In the beginning, success often shows up first as:

- more messages sent

- better replies

- clearer positioning

- stronger conversations

- improved confidence

- a better understanding of objections

Those things matter because they lead to money.

Do not ignore leading indicators just because they are not cash yet.

Constantly changing direction

This is the beginner trap that wastes the most time.

The offer feels uncertain, so you switch.
The niche feels quiet, so you switch.
The first three messages get ignored, so you switch.

Every switch resets your learning.

Stick long enough to gather real evidence.

Setting goals without tracking actions

A money goal without activity targets is just pressure.

You need both.

The result goal gives you direction.
The activity goals give you a way to get there.

Waiting for motivation instead of using a system

Motivation is unreliable when you are tired, stressed, embarrassed, or worried about money.

A system protects you from your moods.

That is why daily numbers matter so much. They give you a structure to lean on when your confidence dips.

Quick Win Task

Open a notebook, notes app, or spreadsheet and write this heading:

My First $1,000 Plan

Then fill in these lines:

- My offer:
- My audience:
- My price:
- My $1,000 path:
- My daily outreach target:
- My daily follow-up target:
- My weekly sample goal:
- My review day:

Then send your first 10 messages today.

Not until you feel more ready.
Not after you polish everything.
Not after one more tutorial.

Today.

That first set of messages matters more than another hour of preparation.

Because action creates clarity.
Action creates feedback.
And feedback is what gets you paid.

Your first $1,000 no longer has to feel mysterious.

It is not some magical milestone reserved for people who are more confident, more polished, or more naturally "good at business."

It is usually built in a much less dramatic way.

One offer.
One audience.
A price that makes sense.
A daily number of messages.
A habit of following up.
A simple tracker.
A willingness to stay with the process long enough for it to work.

That is the real story behind most first wins.

Not a genius.
Not luck.
Not perfect timing.

Just clear numbers and steady action.

And maybe that is the most encouraging part.

Because if the first $1,000 came down to talent alone, a lot of people would be stuck. But if it comes down to choosing a path, doing the work, and learning as you go, then this is something ordinary people can actually do.

Including you.

So stop asking whether this can work in theory.

Pick the target.
Set the numbers.
Run the days.

Track the truth.

Keep going.

The first $1,000 is not earned by the person who feels ready.

It is earned by the person who keeps showing up long enough to make the numbers real.

Chapter 11: Turn a One-Time Win into Ongoing Income

The first time someone pays you for AI-assisted work, something shifts.

It may not be a huge amount. It might be $40, $75, or $150. It may not solve your money problems. You may still have bills stacked on the counter, a rent payment coming up, or that familiar stress that hits when you check your balance.

But the emotional impact is bigger than the number.

Because before that first payment, this whole idea can feel shaky. You are hoping it works. Testing things. Watching other people talk about making money online and wondering whether they know something you do not. You are not sure if you are too late, too inexperienced, too unqualified, or just kidding yourself.

Then someone pays you.

And now it is no longer a fantasy. It is evidence.

That first sale matters because it answers the question that has been quietly haunting you: **Can I actually do this for real?**

Yes. You can.

Now comes the part most beginners miss.

Getting one client is exciting. Turning that one client into repeat income is what changes your month. That is what starts to calm the panic. That is what moves you from random wins to something you can build on.

This chapter is about that shift.

Not how to chase endless new ideas.
Not how to work harder for the same money.
Not how to stay stuck starting from zero every week.

This is about how to turn one small win into something bigger.

Reality Check

Let's be honest: one-off income is encouraging, but it is also unstable.

A client hires you for one résumé.
A business buys one set of captions.
A seller asks for a handful of product descriptions.
A creator pays you once to repurpose a video.

That is a good start. But if every week begins with, "I need to find someone new," you will feel like you are running on a treadmill. You are moving, but never fully catching up.

That kind of income keeps you in a fragile state.

You feel pressure to say yes to every job.
You keep your prices low because you are afraid of losing people.
You jump to new methods too quickly because you want something

easier.

You spend more time hunting than building.

That is not a business. That is survival mode.

And survival mode makes everything feel harder than it needs to be.

The better move is usually not to go wider. It is to go deeper with what already worked.

If someone trusted you once, that matters.
If your work helped them, that matters even more.
If they still have related problems you can solve, that is where ongoing income begins.

You do not need five income streams right now.

You need one simple service that works well enough to repeat.

That is how your first $100 becomes $300.
How $300 becomes $700.
How $700 becomes your first $1,000.

Not through magic. Through extension.

Solution Breakdown

Why the first $1,000 matters psychologically and practically

Your first $1,000 isn't life-changing in some dramatic movie-scene kind of way. For most people, it does not suddenly remove all pressure. But it does something powerful in both your mind and your real life.

Psychologically, it changes your identity.

One small payment can feel like luck. A few payments can still feel like a coincidence. But when you reach your first $1,000, even in smaller pieces, you start to believe something new: **this is not random anymore.**

That matters.

Confidence rarely appears out of nowhere. It usually comes from evidence. From repetition. From seeing that what you did once can be done again.

Practically, the first $1,000 gives you breathing room.

Maybe it covers groceries.
Maybe it pays part of your rent.
Maybe it buys you time.
Maybe it stops that desperate feeling that makes you grab at every shiny new idea.

It also teaches you a lesson many beginners learn too late:

The goal is not to keep proving you can make money once.
The goal is to build something that does not reset to zero every Monday morning.

That is the real value of the first $1,000. It is not just money. It is proof of repeatability.

How to turn buyers into repeat clients

Most people focus all their energy on getting the first sale. That makes sense. The first sale is hard because you are asking someone to trust you without much proof.

But once someone has paid you and had a good experience, the next sale is often much easier.

Why?

Because trust is already there.

They have seen that you communicate.
They have seen that you deliver.
They have seen that you care enough to do the work properly.

You are no longer a stranger.

That means your job is not to "sell harder." Your job is to notice what they are likely to need next and make it easy for them to say yes.

A client almost never thinks in terms of services. They think in terms of problems.

They do not think, "I need a new upsell."
They think, "I still need help with this."

So ask yourself:

What is the next problem that naturally appears after the work I just finished?

If you wrote a résumé, the client may still need help with applying, updating LinkedIn, or writing cover letters.

If you created captions for a small business, they probably still need content next month.

If you rewrote product descriptions, they may still need better titles, tags, and listing structure.

If you repurposed a video into posts, they may still need newsletters, emails, or weekly content support.

Repeat work usually does not come from pushing. It comes from paying attention.

Creating simple monthly packages

A monthly package is just a repeated solution to a repeated problem.

That is all.

Do not overcomplicate it.

A beginner often hears "monthly package" and imagines something big, corporate, and polished. But a monthly package can be very simple.

For example:

A salon owner does not need "content strategy consulting."
They may simply need:

- 12 captions per month
- 4 post ideas
- 1 round of revisions

A job seeker does not need a "career acceleration suite."

They may simply need:

- résumé update

- 2 cover letters per month

- LinkedIn edits when needed

An Etsy seller does not need "brand growth optimisation."

They may simply need:

- 10 new product descriptions

- title rewrites

- listing check-ups for new items

The point is not to sound impressive. The point is to make the offer easy to understand.

A strong monthly package has four qualities:

It solves a recurring problem.

It is easy to explain.

It is realistic for you to deliver.

It saves the client time, stress, or mental energy.

That last part matters most.

People do not buy monthly help because they love paying for services. They buy it because they are tired of dealing with the same problem again and again.

Adding upsells without being pushy

A lot of good people avoid upsells because they do not want to sound salesy.

That is understandable. Especially if you are already uncomfortable charging for your work, the idea of offering more can make you feel greedy.

But a useful upsell is not pressure. It is guidance.

If you can clearly see a next step that would help the client achieve better results, mentioning it is part of doing your job well.

The key is this: the upsell must match the original goal.

If someone paid you to improve their résumé, offering LinkedIn support makes sense. Offering logo design does not.

If someone bought social captions, offering a monthly caption package makes sense. Offering podcast editing probably does not.

A good upsell sounds natural. It feels like this:

"I noticed one thing that would strengthen this even more…"

That sentence works because it comes from observation, not pressure.

Here are a few examples.

For a résumé client:
"Your résumé is much stronger now. The next thing that would help is a matching cover letter for the roles you're applying to. I can do that too if you'd like."

For a small business:

"These captions are ready to go. One thing that might make this easier for you next month is planning the next batch in advance. I can turn this into a simple monthly package if helpful."

For an online seller:

"I finished the descriptions, and I also noticed a few product titles could be improved. That would likely make the listings clearer and stronger. Happy to help with that too."

That is not pushy. That is useful.

Raising prices when your confidence grows

Most beginners underprice at first. That is normal.

You want your first few wins. You want proof. You want to make it easy for someone to say yes. There is nothing wrong with using a lower starting price to build momentum.

The mistake is staying there too long.

At first, a low price feels safe. Later, it starts to cost you.

You begin spending too much time for too little money.
You attract clients who want the cheapest option, not the best help.
You start feeling resentful every time a message comes in.
You get busier, but not more stable.

That is when you know the price is no longer helping you.

Here is a better way to think about pricing:

Your starting price is training wheels. It helps you get moving. But you are not meant to ride with it forever.

Raise your prices when the work is getting easier to deliver, when your results are getting better, and when you have proof that people value what you do.

This does not need to be dramatic.

A résumé service can move from $50 to $75.
A caption pack can move from $100 to $150.
A listing rewrite offer can move from $80 to $120.

Small increases are enough.

And here is the part people rarely say out loud: confidence usually comes after you raise your prices, not before.

You raise them. A few people still say yes. You realise the world did not end. Then your confidence catches up.

Building a tiny portfolio from early work

You do not need a polished website to look legitimate.

You need proof that you can help.

That proof can be simple.

A tiny portfolio might include:

- one before-and-after résumé sample
- a few social caption examples
- a small batch of rewritten product descriptions

- a sample of content turned into posts and a short email
- screenshots of client feedback
- two short testimonials
- a one-page list of your offers

That is enough to start.

Do not wait until it is beautiful. Beautiful is not the standard. Clear is the standard.

A potential client wants reassurance. They want to see that you understand the kind of work they need and that you can produce something solid.

That is what your portfolio is for.

Think of it as a trust builder, not a branding exercise.

Using testimonials to increase trust

Testimonials do one job: they lower the fear in the buyer's mind.

When a stranger is considering hiring you, they are asking themselves questions like:

Will this person actually do what they promised?
Will I waste my money?
Will this be awkward?
Will I have to micromanage them?

A short, honest testimonial helps answer those questions better than a long sales pitch.

You do not need fancy testimonials full of dramatic language. You need believable ones.

Good testimonials sound real.

"This helped me feel much more confident applying for jobs."
"The captions saved me a lot of time each week."
"My listings sound much clearer now."
"She was easy to work with and delivered exactly what I needed."

Those work because they feel human.

Ask for testimonials after a positive result, while the experience is still fresh.

You can say:

"I'm so glad this helped. Would you be open to writing 2–3 sentences about your experience? It would really help me as I build this."

Make it easy. Most people are happy to help if you ask clearly.

Creating systems so delivery gets faster over time

At the start, every project feels like reinventing the wheel.

You have to think through every step.
You second-guess your process.
You waste time deciding what to ask, how to structure the work, and how to deliver it.

That is normal in the beginning. But it should not stay that way.

The more often you repeat a type of job, the more pieces you should standardise.

This is how you stop being overwhelmed and start becoming efficient.

Create:

- a short client questionnaire
- a checklist for each service
- saved prompt templates
- a revision policy
- a delivery format you can reuse
- a testimonial request message
- a follow-up message for future work

These systems may sound boring, but they are what make your income easier to maintain.

Imagine two people both charging $100 for the same kind of work.

One spends four hours on each job because they are scrambling every time.

The other spends ninety minutes because they have a clear process.

Same price. Very different reality.

Speed without chaos is one of the biggest advantages you can build.

When to specialise vs stay flexible

In the early stage, it is fine to stay somewhat open.

You are still learning what sells.

You are still learning what you enjoy.

You are still learning where your strengths actually are.

So yes, early flexibility is useful.

But there is a line between flexibility and confusion.

If your offers are all related, that is fine.

If your offers are all over the place, it becomes hard for people to understand what you do.

For example, this is flexible:

résumés, LinkedIn profiles, cover letters, and job-search support

This is scattered:

résumés, captions, product listings, logo design, websites, virtual assistance, and YouTube thumbnails

The second version makes it harder to build trust because there is no clear lane.

You do not need to specialise immediately. But once one service type starts delivering results more often than the others, pay attention.

Specialise when:

- One offer is easier to sell
- One kind of client is easier to work with
- One service gives better results
- One process feels more repeatable
- One lane has stronger potential for recurring work

That is usually your signal.

You can always expand later. But early on, clarity beats variety.

Step-by-Step Action Plan

Now let's turn this into something practical.

Step 1: Look at your most recent paid job

Do not rush past your early win. Study it.

Ask yourself:
What did the client really want?
What part seemed most valuable to them?
What related problem do they still have?
Could they need this again next month or during the next phase of the same problem?

You are looking for the unfinished need.

That is where your next offer lives.

Step 2: Write the next logical offer in one sentence

Keep this simple.

Use this formula:

Now that I helped with [first job], the next thing I can help with is [next step].

Examples:

Now that I helped with the résumé, the next thing I can help with is a cover letter and LinkedIn update.

Now that I have helped with captions, the next thing I can help with is a monthly content package.

Now that I have helped with product descriptions, the next thing I can help with is title and listing optimisation.

This sentence gives you direction. It stops you from guessing.

Step 3: Message the client without overthinking it

You do not need a perfect script. You need a natural message.

Use this structure:

- thank them
- mention the work you completed
- point out the next useful step
- make the offer feel optional, not pressured

Here is an example for a résumé client:

"I'm really glad I got to help with your résumé. Now that it's in better shape, I think the next step could be a matching cover letter and a cleaner LinkedIn summary. If that would make your applications easier, I can put together a simple package for you."

For a small business:

"I enjoyed working on those captions. Looking at your content, I think it would probably save you time to have a full month planned at once instead of doing it post by post. I can help with that if you want."

For a seller:

"I finished the descriptions and noticed a few listings would be stronger with clearer titles and tags, too. That's something I can help with as a next step if useful."

That is enough. No pressure. No performance.

Step 4: Turn your follow-up into a clear package

Write down:

- what is included
- how many items or how often
- turnaround time
- price

Example:

Monthly Content Support

12 captions

4 content ideas

1 round of edits

Delivered every month

$150

Or:

Job Search Support Package

Résumé update

1 cover letter

LinkedIn summary

Delivered in 4 days

$95

That is your package.

Not vague. Not bloated. Just clear.

Step 5: Save proof from every project

Start building a habit here.

After each job, save:

- a sample of the work
- before-and-after versions if possible
- positive messages from the client
- anything measurable or clearly improved
- a testimonial if they are happy

Create one folder for this.

You are not "getting around to" building a portfolio someday. You are building it one project at a time.

That is how it actually happens in real life.

Step 6: Build your delivery system

For each service you want to keep offering, create the following:

A question list: what you need from the client

A work checklist: your process from start to finish

Saved prompts: what you use with AI to speed things up

A delivery format: how you package the final work

A follow-up template: how you ask about next steps or testimonials

This may take an hour or two to set up, but it saves far more than that later.

Systems reduce stress. They also make you look more professional.

Step 7: Review your pricing after a few successful jobs

Do this after three to five similar projects.

Ask:

Am I delivering faster now?

Do clients seem happy with the results?

Am I getting a yes without much resistance?

Do I have proof that this service works?

Am I starting to feel underpaid?

If the answer is yes, increase your price a little.

Do not apologise for it.

Do not overexplain.

Just update the number and keep going.

Step 8: Choose one lane to strengthen

Once you have a few projects behind you, look at the pattern.

Which service has?

- The smoothest delivery?
- The clearest demand?

- The best client feedback?

- The strongest chance of repeat work?

That is the service to lean into.

You are not marrying it forever. You are just giving yourself a cleaner growth path instead of staying scattered.

Real-World Growth Paths

Here is what this looks like in everyday situations.

From one résumé job to a job-search support package

Imagine you help someone rewrite their résumé for $60.

They are relieved because, for the first time in months, they feel like their application actually reflects who they are. A few days later, they message you again. They have found a job posting they want to apply to and ask whether you can help with the cover letter, too.

This is the moment where many beginners stay small. They quote one more one-off price and move on.

A better move is to zoom out.

This person does not just need a résumé. They need help getting through a stressful job search.

So you create a simple package:

- résumé update

- cover letter

- LinkedIn summary

- optional edits for a second application

Now you are no longer selling a single document. You are supporting a result the client actually cares about: getting interviews.

That is a stronger offer and a more natural reason for them to stay with you.

From social captions to monthly content support

A small business owner hires you for one batch of captions.

Maybe it is a hair salon, a local café, a fitness coach, or a dog groomer. They like what you send, but what they really love is not just the writing. It is the relief.

For once, they do not have to sit there staring at Instagram trying to think of what to say.

That relief is the real value.

So instead of waiting for them to come back randomly, you offer monthly support:

- 12 captions
- 4 monthly post ideas
- promo hooks for events or offers
- one revision round

Now your service solves an ongoing problem, not a one-time task.

That is how you move from "freelance gig" to "steady client."

From product descriptions to full listing optimisation

An Etsy or Shopify seller hires you to rewrite a few product descriptions.

As you work, you notice other issues too. Their titles are weak. Their listings are inconsistent. Their products sound plain when they should sound desirable.

This is where your value grows.

You can now offer:

- product description rewrites
- title improvements
- clearer feature or benefit formatting
- simple tag or keyword suggestions
- shop-wide consistency support

What started as basic writing becomes a fuller optimisation service.

The client does not care what you call it. They care that their listings look stronger and sell more clearly.

From repurposing content to newsletter and email support

A creator hires you to turn one video into a few social posts.

You do the job, but then you notice something useful: the same content could also become a newsletter, an email, or a short sequence promoting their offer.

Many creators and small business owners are sitting on content they are not fully using. They post once and move on. That is where your opportunity is.

So your next offer becomes:

- social posts from weekly content
- one newsletter draft
- one promotional email
- content repurposing across platforms

This is valuable because it helps them stay visible without constantly creating from scratch.

And the more of their workflow you support, the more likely they are to keep coming back.

Common Mistakes to Avoid

Staying underpriced too long

Low prices can help you get started. But after a while, they stop being a strategy and start being fear.

You tell yourself you will raise prices later.
Later turns into months.
Months turn into resentment.

The result is that you work hard, stay busy, and still feel stuck.

Start low if you need to. Do not stay low because you are scared.

Chasing new methods before stabilising one

This is one of the biggest reasons beginners never gain traction.

They make a little money writing captions, then drop it to try affiliate marketing.

Then they hear about selling prompts.
Then they switch to printables.
Then they try faceless videos.
Then they start over again.

It feels productive because there is always motion. But the income remains inconsistent because nothing matures long enough.

A working offer often looks boring before it looks valuable.

Stay with it long enough to build proof, systems, and repeat business.

Saying yes to every type of client

When money is tight, every opportunity feels important. That can make you too open.

You take unclear jobs.
You agree to bad prices.
You accept clients who are demanding, vague, or exhausting.

At first, some trial and error is normal. But pay attention to the clients and projects that leave you drained.

The goal is not just to get paid. The goal is to get paid for work you can repeat without dreading it.

Neglecting repeat business while chasing new leads

Many beginners overlook the easiest money available to them: people who have already said yes once.

They spend hours trying to convince strangers while ignoring past clients who already know they are reliable.

Do not make that mistake.

Before you go searching for brand-new leads, ask:
Who have I already helped?
What might they need next?
Have I followed up?

That question alone can bring in income faster than a week of cold outreach.

Quick Win Task

Do this today.

Not later. Not when you feel more prepared. Today.

Open a note and write these five lines:

1. The last thing someone paid me for was:

2. The next thing they are likely to need is:

3. I can turn that into this package:

4. My follow-up message will say:

5. The proof I can save from that project is:

Then send one follow-up message.

Just one.

That single message may lead to your next client payment, your first package, your first testimonial, or your first repeat customer.

Small actions like this are how income begins to feel real.

A one-time win is encouraging. But ongoing income is what changes your life.

Not because it makes you rich overnight. It probably will not.

But because repeated income does something deeply calming. It softens the constant panic. It gives you a little space to think. It helps you stop feeling like every week is an emergency.

That kind of relief matters more than people admit.

If money has been tight for a while, what you want most is not hype. It is stability. A little predictability. A sense that you are not always one bad week away from falling behind again.

That is why this chapter matters.

Your first client is not just a payment.
It is proof.
It is practice.
It is a sample.
It is a testimonial waiting to happen.
It is a referral opportunity.
It is the beginning of a process you can improve.

Do not treat your first win like a lucky break and move on.

Study it.
Build on it.
Extend it.
Package it.
Systemise it.

Ask for the next step.

Raise the value.

Save the proof.

That is how a small start becomes something steady.

Not all at once.

Not perfectly.

But piece by piece.

And that is enough.

Because when you have been worried about money for a long time, "piece by piece" is not disappointing.

It is how you finally begin to climb out.

Chapter 12: Build an AI Income Stream You Can Trust

Making your first $1,000 with AI can feel like a miracle when money has been tight.

For a moment, the pressure lifts. You look at your phone or your bank balance and think, *Wait... I actually did that.* Not by winning the lottery. Not by getting rescued. Not by suddenly becoming a tech expert. You solved a problem, someone paid you, and now something that felt far away feels real.

That moment matters.

But here is the part nobody talks about enough: the first $1,000 is exciting because it gives you hope. The next $1,000 matters even more because it teaches you whether you can trust yourself to do it again.

That is the difference between a lucky break and a new direction for your life.

A quick win feels good. A dependable income stream changes how you sleep, how you think, how you handle bills, and how you see your future. It gives you something most financially stressed people have not felt in a long time:

A little control.

This chapter is about building that. Not a flashy business. Not a fake online empire. Not a complicated system that looks impressive but falls apart in real life. Something smaller, steadier, and more useful than that.

An AI income stream you can trust.

One that still works when motivation drops.
One that does not depend on panic.
One that protects your reputation.
One that grows because it is built on real value, not noise.

If the first money gave you belief, this chapter will help you build stability.

Reality Check

Let's tell the truth about what happens after the first success.

Many beginners make a little money once and assume they have "made it." The following week is quiet. No replies. No sales. No new clients. Suddenly, that exciting first win feels fragile. They wonder whether it was just luck. They start second-guessing everything. They jump to a different tool, niche, offer, or strategy.

That is how people accidentally turn progress into chaos.

The real problem is not that they failed. The real problem is that they tried to build something stable on top of random effort.

A quick win is not the same thing as a reliable income stream.

A quick win is one résumé job from a friend's referral.
A sustainable income stream is a simple service that consistently generates work.

A quick win is selling one pack of captions to a local business.
A sustainable income stream is turning that into monthly content support.

A quick win proves someone will pay.
A sustainable stream proves you know how to create value more than once.

That shift matters because financial stress does strange things to people. It makes you impatient. It makes every slow day feel like danger. It makes you want to chase every opportunity, say yes to everything, buy tools too early, copy people you do not even want to become, and overwork just to feel safe.

That reaction is understandable. But it is not sustainable.

You do not need more chaos dressed up as ambition. You need a process you can repeat.

And you do not need to learn everything.

This is where many people get stuck. They think the answer is to become "better at AI" in a broad, endless way. So they keep consuming videos, prompts, hacks, tools, newsletters, and tutorials. They become busy, but not useful. Informed, but not paid.

The goal is not to learn everything AI can do.

The goal is to get very good at using AI to solve a small set of real problems for real people.

That is how trust is built.
That is how income becomes steadier.
That is how your first win stops feeling like an accident.

Solution Breakdown

The difference between a quick win and a sustainable income stream

Think of a quick win as proof. Think of a sustainable income stream as a structure.

Proof is exciting, but structure is what changes your life.

A quick win tells you, "This is possible."
A sustainable income stream tells you, "I know how to do this again."

That second sentence is where confidence starts to become real.

Imagine a woman named Tasha. She helps one job seeker improve a résumé using AI and earns $85. She is thrilled. But instead of stopping there, she pays attention. She notices that the client also needed a cover letter, LinkedIn help, and interview answers. She realises the problem was never "just a résumé." The real problem was that this person felt lost and needed job-search support.

So Tasha makes a smarter offer:
résumé rewrite, cover letter, LinkedIn summary, and a short interview prep sheet.

Then she creates a repeatable process. A short intake form. A checklist. A saved prompt for drafting. A final review step before delivery. Now she is not just hoping another random résumé request appears. She has turned one small success into a service people can understand, buy, and recommend.

That is the shift.

A sustainable income stream usually has three traits:

It solves a recurring problem
it gets easier for you to deliver over time.
It creates chances for repeat work, referrals, or package upgrades.

If your offer only works once, with one type of person, in one lucky situation, it may make money, but it will be hard to rely on.

If your offer can be packaged, repeated, improved, and sold again, now you are building something.

How to keep learning without getting overwhelmed

One of the easiest ways to stall your progress is to turn learning into a hiding place.

It feels responsible. It feels productive. It feels safer than putting yourself out there. But too much learning at the wrong time becomes a form of procrastination with better branding.

You do not need to master AI.

You need to use it well enough to do paid work responsibly.

That means your learning should follow your income, not replace it.

Learn in this order:

First, learn what helps you deliver your current offer well.
Then, learn what helps you deliver it faster.
Then, learn what helps you charge more for it.

That order matters.

If you are getting paid to write product descriptions for Etsy sellers, the next useful thing to learn might be how to capture a product's tone better, how to write stronger first lines, or how to create a faster workflow. It is probably not learning ten new tools you may never use.

If you are helping job seekers, you may need to get better at tailoring documents to specific roles, writing sharper LinkedIn summaries, or asking better intake questions. You do not need to become an expert in every branch of AI.

A good question to ask each week is:

"What slowed me down or weakened my results this week?"

Then learn only enough to fix that.

This keeps you grounded in real work instead of endless possibilities.

Using profits wisely: reinvest, save, and reduce pressure

When you have been under financial pressure for a long time, your first instinct is often to use any new money to put out fires. That makes sense. Sometimes you need to. Rent is real. Food is real. Bills are real.

But if every dollar that comes in disappears instantly, your new income stream stays emotionally fragile. You never get the benefit of breathing room. You never reduce desperation. You never build the kind of stability that helps you make better decisions.

That is why early profits need a job.

A simple way to think about it is this:

Use some money to live.
Use some money to protect yourself.
Use some money to strengthen the work.

That may look like this:

A portion goes to immediate needs.
A portion goes into savings, even if it is small.
A portion goes back into tools, systems, or support that help you earn more easily.

You do not need perfect percentages. You need intention.

Maybe your first $300 after expenses means:
some groceries, a small emergency cushion, and one paid tool that saves you two hours a week.

Maybe it means:

paying a bill, putting aside enough to stop panicking for three days, and buying a domain or portfolio template.

The amount matters less than the habit.

The deeper reason this matters is psychological. When you have no cushion at all, you become easy to pressure. You undercharge. You take bad clients. You rush. You say yes when you should pause. You tolerate disrespect because you need the money too badly.

Even a small buffer can help you think more clearly.

That is not a luxury.
That is protection.

Protecting your reputation in AI-assisted work

Your reputation is one of the few business assets you start building from day one.

And in AI-assisted work, reputation matters even more because people are already cautious. They have seen low-quality output. They have read generic, awkward, obviously machine-written content. They have heard stories about fake experts selling polished nonsense.

So when someone hires you, they are not just buying the result. They are testing whether you can be trusted.

That means you cannot send raw AI output and hope for the best.

You have to review.
You have to think.

You have to notice when something sounds off.

You have to catch mistakes before your client does.

If you are writing captions for a local business, the tone has to fit that business.

If you are rewriting a résumé, the details must be accurate.

If you are helping with product descriptions, the copy cannot sound generic or describe the wrong product.

If you are drafting emails or profiles, the voice must feel human.

AI can help you draft. It cannot care for your reputation. That part is your job.

Picture a beginner named Marcus who offers product descriptions for small online shops. He gets excited when three orders come in and rushes through them. He copies the seller's product details into a tool, skims the output, and sends it over. One listing uses words that do not fit the brand. Another includes features the product does not actually have. The descriptions are not terrible, but they are careless.

The client probably will not say, "Marcus failed to use AI correctly." They will say, "I do not trust this person with my business."

That is the real risk.

Protecting your reputation is not about being perfect. It is about being responsible.

Before you deliver anything, ask:

Is this accurate?

Is it specific to the client?

Does it sound natural?

Would I feel proud if this client forwarded it to someone else?

If not, it is not ready.

Ethical boundaries and transparency

You can build this the right way.

In fact, building it the right way is one of your advantages, because so many people do not.

Ethics in AI-assisted work do not need to be dramatic or complicated. Most of the time, it comes down to honesty, boundaries, and basic respect.

Do not claim skills you do not have.
Do not promise outcomes you cannot control.
Do not pretend careless work is customised.
Do not plagiarise.
Do not use client information recklessly.
Do not fake testimonials or results.
Do not take on work where mistakes could seriously harm someone if you are not qualified.

That last point matters more than people think.

Helping a bakery write better Instagram captions is one thing. Pretending you can handle legal documents, medical advice, immigration paperwork, or financial planning just because AI can generate words is something else entirely.

Stay in lanes where your judgment is strong enough to protect the client.

Transparency matters too. That does not mean you need to overexplain every tool you use. It means your positioning should be honest.

You can say things like:

"I use AI-assisted drafting and then manually customise and review the final version."

Or:

"I use AI to speed up research and first drafts, but I edit for clarity, tone, and accuracy."

That is honest, professional, and reassuring. It tells the client you are using technology as a tool, not as an excuse to care less.

A useful test is this:

If the client saw exactly how I created this, would they feel respected or misled?

Build in a way that lets you answer that question with confidence.

When to upgrade tools, skills, and offers

A lot of beginners upgrade too early because upgrading feels like progress.

A new tool feels exciting.

A new service feels ambitious.

A new course feels responsible.

A new niche feels strategic.

Sometimes those moves help. Often, they are just expensive ways to avoid mastering the basics.

You do not need more until the current version of your work has started to strain under real demand.

Upgrade tools when a tool clearly saves time, improves quality, or removes repeated frustration in work you are already doing.

Upgrade skills when a better skill would help you get stronger results, reduce revisions, or make the same service more valuable.

Upgrade offers when clients keep asking for related help, or when your current service has a natural next step that people are ready to buy.

Do not upgrade because you are bored.

Do not upgrade because someone on the internet made you feel behind.

Do not upgrade because complexity makes you feel more legitimate.

Upgrade when the evidence says it is time.

For example:

If three clients in a row ask whether you also offer LinkedIn optimisation, that may be a sign to expand a résumé offer.

If writing captions takes too long because your workflow is messy, that may be the moment to pay for a better tool or organise your prompt system.

If your clients keep coming back each month for new work, that may be the right time to create a retainer.

Growth works best when it follows demand, not insecurity.

Creating a simple weekly routine for ongoing income

A trustworthy income stream usually does not come from bursts of motivation. It comes from rhythm.

A simple weekly routine protects you from two extremes that hurt beginners: panic and drift.

Panic says, "I have to do everything right now."
Drift says, "I will do something later."

A weekly routine gives your effort shape.

At a minimum, your week should include five things:

Reaching out,
Following up,
Delivering client work,
Improving one part of your process,
and handling the boring admin that keeps things clean.

That is enough.

You do not need a colour-coded productivity system. You need a rhythm you can keep even when life is messy.

For example:

One day for outreach.
One day for follow-up.
A few blocks for delivery.
A short block for improving templates or prompts.
A short block for organising payments, files, and client messages.

Simple beats impressive here. Always.

Expanding into bigger opportunities

Once one offer works, you do not need to start over to grow. You can expand from where you already have trust.

That is the smartest kind of growth.

Retainers

Retainers are ongoing monthly agreements where a client pays you regularly for continued support.

This is one of the best ways to stabilise your income. Instead of constantly hunting for new one-off projects, you keep a few steady clients.

A person who buys captions once may need them every month.
A job seeker may want support for the next 30 days.
A small shop owner may need new product descriptions regularly.
A creator may want weekly content help.

Retainers reduce the emotional whiplash of starting from zero every week.

Digital products

Digital products let you sell something more than once without redoing the work from scratch each time.

This could be a résumé template pack, a job-seeker prompt guide, a caption bundle for real estate agents, a simple client intake template, or a product description worksheet.

Digital products usually work best after you have done enough client work to know what people actually need. They should come from experience, not guesswork.

A good digital product often begins with something you have already repeated many times.

Micro-agencies

A micro-agency sounds bigger than it needs to be.

In practice, it can be very small. It might simply mean that you bring in one trusted freelancer to help with delivery when demand grows. Maybe you handle client communication and strategy while someone else helps with formatting, editing, research, or design.

This can help when your bottleneck is no longer getting clients. It is capacity.

You do not need to rush into this. But it becomes useful when you have more demand than your schedule can handle alone.

Niche specialization

Specialisation means becoming known for solving one kind of problem for one kind of person.

That makes you easier to trust, easier to remember, and easier to recommend.

"AI help" is vague.
"LinkedIn and résumé support for job seekers" is clear.
"Product descriptions for handmade Etsy shops" is clear.
"Monthly social captions for local service businesses" is clear.

You do not have to pick a forever niche immediately. But over time, it is wise to notice where your work gets the best response, where results come more easily, and what kind of clients you actually enjoy serving.

Specialisation often emerges from experience. You do not force it too early. You pay attention until it reveals itself.

What the second $1,000 teaches you

The first $1,000 proves you can make money.
The second $1,000 teaches you how your business actually works.

That is a huge difference.

By the time you earn the second round, patterns start showing up.

You begin to notice which offers are easier to sell.
Which clients pay the fastest?
Which projects drain too much time?
Which messages get responses?

Which revisions happen over and over?

Which parts of the delivery should have been templated weeks ago?

This is valuable information.

The second $1,000 teaches you that income is not only about effort. It is about awareness. It shows you where your process is weak, where your value is strongest, and what kind of work is worth building around.

It also teaches something more personal.

It teaches you whether you can stay steady after the excitement wears off.

Because almost anyone can feel motivated after a first win.
The real growth happens when you can keep going without the adrenaline.

Why this is bigger than money: control, confidence, and freedom

Money matters. When you are struggling, it matters a lot.

It pays for food, rent, transport, school costs, debt payments, medicine, and moments of relief that should not feel luxurious but often do.

But the deeper shift is not just in your bank account. It is in your identity.

You stop seeing yourself as someone who can only survive by hoping things improve.

You start seeing yourself as someone who can create value on purpose.

That changes you.

You walk differently when you know you can earn.
You think differently when you know you can solve problems.
You recover from setbacks differently when you know you are not powerless.

That is why this matters more than the money itself.

The money eases pressure.
The skill gives you leverage.
The proof gives you confidence.
The process gives you freedom.

Not total freedom all at once. Real life is not that simple. But even a little more control can change the way a person lives.

And for many people, that is where the rebuilding begins.

Step-by-Step Action Plan

Now let's turn this into something you can actually use.

Step 1: Choose one offer that has repeat potential

Pick one service that solves a problem people commonly have.

Not five offers. One.

It might be:
a résumé and cover letter package,

a LinkedIn rewrite,

a batch of social captions,

product descriptions for online sellers,

email support for small businesses,

or blog repurposing for creators.

The offer should be clear enough that someone can understand it in one sentence.

Write this down:

"I help ___ get ___ by providing ___."

Examples:

"I help job seekers get stronger applications by rewriting résumés, cover letters, and LinkedIn profiles."

"I help small business owners stay visible online by creating ready-to-post caption packs."

"I help Etsy sellers improve listings by writing clear, persuasive product descriptions."

If you cannot explain it simply, it is still too vague.

Step 2: Turn that offer into a repeatable process

Open a blank document and write down your full workflow from start to finish.

Keep it simple.

For example:

Client asks about the service.

I sent a short explanation and price.

I collect details with a few intake questions.

Client sends material or background.

I create a first draft using AI support.

I edit manually for tone, accuracy, and clarity.

I do a final check.

I sent the finished work cleanly.

I ask for feedback.

I request a testimonial if they are happy.

That list may not look impressive, but it is the beginning of stability. Once your work has steps, it becomes easier to improve, faster to deliver, and less mentally exhausting.

Step 3: Build one reusable tool for yourself

Pick one thing that will save time every week.

It could be:

an intake form,

a checklist before delivery,

a saved message for follow-ups,

a short service guide,

a pricing menu,

or a library of prompts you have tested and improved.

Do not try to build a whole system in one day.

Build one useful piece.

A person with five simple reusable assets often works more calmly than a person with ten random ideas in their head.

Step 4: Set a quality standard before every delivery

Create a five-point review checklist for your work.

Before you send anything, ask:

Is this accurate?
Is this tailored to the client?
Does it sound natural and human?
Did I remove weak or generic phrasing?
Is the formatting clean and easy to use?

This takes a few extra minutes, but it saves trust.

Sloppy work creates hidden costs: refunds, awkward conversations, lost referrals, damaged confidence, and the feeling that you are constantly one mistake away from losing momentum.

Step 5: Decide how you will use incoming money

Even if your income is still small, decide now how payments will be handled.

A simple plan might be:

Most goes to current needs,
Some goes into a savings buffer,
Some goes toward business improvement.

You are training yourself to treat this income like something worth protecting, not random cash that appears and disappears.

That habit will help you long before the amounts become bigger.

Step 6: Create a weekly rhythm

Set a basic routine you can repeat.

Example:

Monday: outreach
Tuesday: client work
Wednesday: follow-ups
Thursday: delivery and admin
Friday: improve one part of your process and plan next week

You can adjust this to fit your life. The point is not perfection. The point is consistency.

A routine reduces decision fatigue. It keeps momentum alive when emotions fluctuate.

Step 7: Keep learning narrowly

At the end of each week, write down the answer to these two questions:

What part of the work felt hardest this week?
What one skill or improvement would make next week easier?

Then learn only that.

This keeps your learning practical and prevents overwhelm.

Step 8: Expand only from evidence

Once you have done enough work to spot patterns, grow in the direction that is already working.

If clients keep coming back, create a retainer.
If you keep repeating the same advice, turn it into a digital product.
If one niche responds best, focus on that niche.
If you are too busy delivering, consider light support from another freelancer.

Do not expand because it sounds exciting.
Expand because the work itself is pointing you there.

Common Mistakes to Avoid

One of the biggest mistakes is mistaking one success for a whole business. A first sale is encouraging, but it is not yet stable. Treat it as proof, not a finished system.

Another mistake is hiding inside endless learning. It is easier to watch another tutorial than to send another message, follow up with a lead, or ask a client for a testimonial. But the work that feels vulnerable is usually the work that moves your income forward.

A third mistake is relying too heavily on raw AI output. Clients do not pay for speed alone. They pay for judgment, care, and a result they can actually use. If your work sounds generic or includes errors, trust drops fast.

Many people also make the mistake of expanding too early. They add services, buy expensive tools, redesign branding, and start chasing bigger visions before the current offer is even stable. Growth without a foundation creates stress, not success.

Another common problem is weak boundaries. Taking every client, promising too much, replying at all hours, rushing deadlines, and accepting unclear requests can make a small income stream feel much heavier than it needs to be. A trustworthy business is not built only on usefulness. It is also built on clean expectations.

And finally, many people spend every payment immediately and get trapped in urgency. Even a small habit of saving and reinvesting helps break that cycle.

Quick Win Task

Do this today.

Take one sheet of paper or open one blank document and complete these five lines:

My main offer is:
I help __________ get __________ by providing __________.

My process is:
Write the 7 to 10 steps from the first client message to the final delivery.

My quality checklist is:
Write the 5 things you will review before sending work.

My weekly rhythm is:

Choose which days you will use for outreach, follow-up, delivery, and admin.

My money plan is:

Decide what portion of each payment goes to living needs, savings, and reinvestment.

That is it.

Do not underestimate how powerful this is. Most beginners stay stressed because everything lives in their heads. The moment you put your process on paper, your work starts becoming real.

The most important thing you are building is not just income.

You are building trust in your own ability to create it.

That matters deeply when life has felt uncertain for a long time. When money has been inconsistent, hope can feel dangerous. You stop wanting to believe in anything because disappointment is exhausting. You would rather expect nothing than risk your hopes being let down again.

That is why building a dependable income stream matters so much. It is not just about earning more. It is about becoming someone who knows how to respond to pressure with skill instead of panic.

You do not need to become a genius.

You do not need to become an influencer.

You do not need to build a massive company.

You need to become reliable.

Reliable in the way you solve problems.

Reliable in the way you deliver.

Reliable in the way you protect your name.

Reliable in the way you keep going.

That kind of reliability becomes confidence.

And confidence becomes freedom.

Not the fantasy version of freedom people sell online.

The real version.

The freedom to handle a bill without spiralling.

The freedom to say no to work that feels wrong.

The freedom to believe that you can create money again because you have done it before and built a process around it now.

Your first $1,000 was proof.

What you build next is trust.

And trust, once earned from yourself, is hard to lose.

30-Day Action Plan

From Zero to First Income.

One Simple Step at a Time

Week 1: Reset Your Mindset and Choose a Path

Goal: Move from confusion to clarity.

Day 1

- Read the introduction and Chapter 1
- Write down why you need this income
- Define your 30-day financial target

Day 2

- Read Chapter 2
- Eliminate unrealistic methods
- Circle the 3 methods that feel most doable

Day 3

- Read Chapter 3
- Choose one income path only
- Write a one-sentence description of your offer

Day 4

- Research 10 real examples of people or businesses who could use your help
- Notice what problems repeat

Day 5

- Decide your niche and target buyer
- Complete this sentence: "I help ___ get ___ by providing ___"

Day 6

- List the exact result your offer delivers
- Create a simple promise and delivery time

Day 7

- Review your decisions
- Remove anything that feels too broad or complicated

Week 2: Set Up Tools, Samples, and Your Offer

Goal: Become ready to sell something real.

Day 8

- Set up your free tool stack
- Create folders, templates, and a basic workflow

Day 9

- Learn 3–5 useful AI prompt patterns
- Practice on your chosen service

Day 10

- Create your first sample using AI plus human editing
- Focus on clarity, not perfection

Day 11

- Create a second sample in a different style or for a different type of client

Day 12

- Finalise your offer
- Decide price, deliverables, and turnaround time

Day 13

- Write a short service description
- Create a one-page document or message you can send to prospects

Day 14

- Prepare 3 outreach messages
- Build a list of 25 potential buyers

Week 3: Outreach, Conversations, and First Sales

Goal: Start getting responses and opportunities.

Day 15

- Send your first 10 outreach messages
- Track every message sent

Day 16

- Send 10 more
- Follow up with anyone warm or curious

Day 17

- Offer 1–3 mini samples or audits to strong prospects
- Ask simple questions to uncover needs

Day 18

- Continue outreach
- Improve your message based on replies

Day 19

- Aim for your first paid conversation
- Practice explaining your offer in one minute

Day 20

- Handle objections
  - "I'm not ready"
  - "I can do it myself"
  - "I don't have a budget"

- Focus on the value of saving time and getting better results

Day 21

- Push for your first payment or agreement
- If no sale yet, review:
  - Is the audience right?
  - Is the offer clear?
  - Is the price reasonable?
  - Are you reaching enough people?

Week 4: Deliver, Improve, and Reach $1,000

Goal: Turn action into income and repeat it.

Day 22

- Deliver your first job with care
- Ask for feedback and a testimonial

Day 23

- Refine your process
- Save your steps into a repeatable system

Day 24

- Ask your first client for a referral or second task

Day 25

- Send another 10 outreach messages with your improved offer

Day 26

- Raise confidence through proof
- Use testimonials, samples, or results in your messages

Day 27

- Create a simple repeat package or upsell
- Example: one-off captions become monthly content support

Day 28

- Review your numbers
- How much was earned?
- How many offers sent?
- What got the best response?

Day 29

- Double down on the best-performing method
- Cut anything wasting time

Day 30

- Total your results
- Build your 30-day-after-the-30-days plan
- Set your next income target

Conclusion

Your First $1,000 Is Not the Finish Line, It Is the Proof

Key messages for the close

- The biggest transformation is not just financial, it is psychological.
- The reader no longer has to see themselves as "someone who can't".
- They now understand how to create value with simple tools.
- They have proof that action beats perfection.
- They can repeat this process, refine it, and grow it.
- AI did not replace them—it amplified their usefulness.
- The first $1,000 is evidence that a new chapter has begun.

Final emotional payoff

- They are no longer waiting for permission.
- They are no longer trapped in confusion.
- They now have a practical skill stack, a simple income method, and a repeatable plan.
- What started as survival can become self-trust, stability, and freedom.